# J. Krishnamurti Demystified

*Simple explanations of the seer's teachings to help solve the Problems of Human Life*

Dr. Kalidas Joshi
M.Sc., M.A., Ph.D.

PUSTAK MAHAL®
Delhi • Bangalore • Mumbai • Patna • Hyderabad

*Publishers*
**Pustak Mahal®, Delhi-110006**

*Sales Centres*

- 6686, Khari Baoli, Delhi-110006, *Ph:* 23944314, 23911979
- 10-B, Netaji Subhash Marg, Daryaganj, New Delhi-110002
  *Ph:* 23268292, 23268293, 23279900 • *Fax:* 011-23280567
  *E-mail:* rapidexdelhi@indiatimes.com

*Administrative Office*

J-3/16 (Opp. Happy School), Daryaganj, New Delhi-110002
*Ph:* 23276539, 23272783, 23272784 • *Fax:* 011-23260518
*E-mail:* info@pustakmahal.com • *Website:* www.pustakmahal.com

*Branch Offices*

BANGALORE: 22/2, Mission Road (Shama Rao's Compound), Bangalore-560027, *Ph:* 22234025 • *Fax:* 080-22240209
*E-mail*: pmblr@sancharnet.in • pustak@sancharnet.in

MUMBAI: 23-25, Zaoba Wadi (Opp. VIP Showroom), Thakurdwar, Mumbai-400002, *Ph:* 22010941 • *Fax:* 022-22053387
*E-mail*: rapidex@bom5.vsnl.net.in

PATNA: Khemka House, 1st Floor (Opp. Women's Hospital), Ashok Rajpath, Patna-800004, *Ph:* 3094193 • *Telefax:* 0612-2302719
*E-mail*: rapidexptn@rediffmail.com

HYDERABAD: 5-1-707/1, Brij Bhawan, Bank Street, Koti, Hyderabad-500095, *Telefax:* 040-24737290
*E-mail*: pustakmahalhyd@yahoo.co.in



ISBN 81-223-0899-6



**Edition : January 2005**

***Printed at :*** Garg Offset Printers, Delhi

## Dedication

To the Sacred Memory of
Doctor Shyamaprasad Mukerji,
One of the Brightest Sons of Bharatavarsha,
Who Made Supreme Sacrifice for
Our Beloved Motherland

# Preface

My earlier book '**Understanding J. Krishnamurti**' (published in June 2002 by Rupa and Co.) was aimed at considering the main features of the teachings of the sage, so as to (*i*) bring the gist of the whole teachings in one single volume and (*ii*) to make it intelligible and clear to an average educated inquirer. It has been quite a successful book. But it was a learned work, which tried to go into the very root of each of the 14 main themes discussed repeatedly by Krishnamurti. Most of us do not really care to go to such lengths and consider the subtleties involved in the basic problems of life. We do not want to go very deep into the root of the problem. We, the common people, belong to the privileged class. We have the privilege of being very sure of our own beliefs, prejudices, conclusions, likes and dislikes. The present book '**J. Krishnamurti and The Problems of Human Life**' has been written keeping in mind the needs, interests, and peculiarities of this privileged class of common people.

To try and overcome the peculiar obscurity and unintelligibility associated with the teachings of J. Krishnamurti is the main purpose of this book. Our interaction with the sage seems to have some gaps, some missing links. It has been my endeavour in this book to provide these missing links. I have nowhere tried to explain or interpret the statements of the sage, but have just reproduced them without any change whatsoever, for fear of distortion of the teachings in any manner. This is a special feature of the book to be noted clearly.

The book includes 187 different problems of human life, which have been discussed by the sage throughout his life, in different books, which are listed in the Bibliography at the end of the book. First, I have explained each problem in my own words, mentioning different views about it. Then the statements of the sage are given in inverted commas. At the end of each statement, the source is given in brackets in two figures, the first indicating the serial number of the book in the Bibliography, and the second showing the page number where the statement has appeared. The key words used by the sage, which we find difficult to understand, are explained, making their meaning clear. This is the main contribution of the book which makes it possible to overcome the obscurity that has always been an impediment in understanding Krishnamurti adequately and completely.

The book contains four chapters. Each chapter provides information which has so far never been made available anywhere by any writer. In the first chapter, 'Who was J. Krishnamurti?', after describing his life events briefly, eight remarkable characteristics of the sage, which mark him as very different from others, are mentioned. Such a critical estimation is perhaps attempted for the first time in any book on the life and teachings of J. Krishnamurti. The second chapter, 'What Were the Teachings', deals with the attempt to present a broad framework or the main features, the foundations of the whole teachings of the sage spread over a period of fifty-seven years, and contained in over a quarter century of his books. The sage himself never attempted to do that. And of course, none of the writers, who wrote about his teachings, has tried to make such an attempt so far. This second chapter consists of twelve great sayings of the sage, which, it is thought, would form the framework of his whole teachings. These may be called **mahāvākyas**, or **āryasatyas** or the twelve commandments of J. Krishnamurti.

The third chapter deals with the obscurity and unintelligibility associated with the teachings, the reasons for the same, and gives a few examples of passages which are very hard to understand. The fourth chapter, which is the main body of the book, deals with 187 problems of human life in the light of what the sage said about them. The following problems are more important, and one should try to understand them properly. If they are understood clearly, one would understand the teachings of the sage more easily and find it enjoyable, and that would help to bring about an inner change. Thereby, one would benefit immensely from the 'one-of-its-kind' teachings of J. Krishnamurti. Here are those more important problems:

1. Aloneness
2. Anonymity
3. Attention
4. Authority

5. Belief
6. Centre
7. Conditioning
8. Conflict
9. Conformity
10. Death
11. Desire
12. Direct perception
13. Disorder
14. Dying to the past
15. Energy
16. Escapes
17. Fragmentation
18. Freedom
19. Human mind
20. Image
21. Knowing oneself
22. Me
23. Naming
24. Negation
25. Passion
26. Revolution
27. Sorrow
28. What is

After reading this book thoroughly, if one were to read any original book of J. Krishnamurti, it would be enjoyed more clearly and easily, and one would benefit much more from the teachings of the sage. If that does happen, then the purpose of this book would be amply served.

**KALIDAS JOSHI**
Pune

# Contents

# Contents

## Chapter 1

# Who Was J. Krishnamurti?

Jiddu Krishnamurti was, indeed, a unique personality of the twentieth century. He was highly admired as a sage of 'pathless truth', intently heard as a speaker of wisdom, widely read as a writer on death, desire and discovery, yet very poorly and inadequately understood by all who tried in vain for years and decades to actually experience in daily life the wonderful state of deep silence, and of perceiving and comprehending "**what is**", which figured repeatedly in each of his talks and every chapter of his books throughout his life.

He was born in a Telugu Brahmin family in the year 1895, after the sunset of 11$^{th}$ May and before the sunrise of 12$^{th}$ May, at midnight, at a village called Madanapalli, in Chittoor district bordering the states of Andhra Pradesh and Karnataka in south India. He was the eighth among eleven children of Jiddu Narayanaiah and Sanjeevamma. After the death of his mother, when he was ten years of age, the family shifted to Adyar, Madras, now Chennai, where his father joined as an employee of the Theosophical Society, after his retirement from Government service.

Krishnamurti was not a bright boy at school. He was not a very healthy child either. Many a time he was punished by the school teacher for remaining absent from class due to illness and for lagging behind in his studies. Staring far away into space with half-open mouth and blank eyes was his peculiar pastime. The Theosophical Society, its President, Annie Besant, and her confidant Charles Webster Leadbeater, were all to play a major role in the life of J. Krishnamurti very soon. In the year 1909 (possibly in the month of May), he was 'discovered' by Leadbeater while playing with his younger brother Nityananda on the banks of the Adyar river. Leadbeater felt that he was the vehicle in whose body the next world teacher of Theosophy would manifest himself for the liberation of humanity from ignorance and misery. The Theosophical Society was formed in 1874 in America, for preparing humanity to receive the world teacher. The two boys were adopted by Annie Besant. They were taken to England for training in order to prepare them to carry out the divine mission of the world teacher. Krishnamurti underwent several initiations into the esoteric discipline of Theosophy. He used to be taken in his astral body to meet the Masters of Theosophy, who imparted instructions to him that he wrote down after returning to the gross body. Thus came into existence the book '*At the Feet of the Master*', which was translated into several languages and sold millions of copies.

For nearly twenty years from 1909 to 1929, the preparation of J. Krishnamurti to play the role of the world teacher continued. Nityananda, who was to play an important side role in the whole world game, died of tuberculosis in 1925. This was an unbearable shock for the world teacher in the making, who was extremely attached to his younger brother. His mind was shattered completely and his life was in total disarray. The shock ultimately resulted in a revolt against the whole gamut of ideas and activities of Theosophy, and on 3rd August 1929, at the Ommen Camp in Holland, in a grand ceremony meant to launch the world teacher, Krishnamurti declared that "the key to happiness is one's own self; no one holds that key", and that he was not a world teacher.

Subsequently, he severed relations with Theosophy and followed his own separate path for the next fifty-seven years, giving talks in order to "set man absolutely, unconditionally free". From the talks, a number of books in English were prepared. He died from cancer of the pancreas, at the age of 91 years, on 18th February 1986, at Ojai, California, USA.

A detailed account of the life of the sage can be had from the following books:

1. Jaykar, Pupul, *J. Krishnamurti—A Biography*, Harmondsworth; 1986, Penguin Books.
2. Lutyens Mary, *Krishnamurti—The Years of Awakening*, London; 1975, John Murray.

3. Sloss, Radha Rajgopal, *Lives in the Shadow with J. Krishnamurti*, London; 1991, Bloomsbury Publishers Ltd.

More information on the life of the sage is also given in my earlier book, *Understanding J. Krishnamurti*, Rupa and Co.

J. Krishnamurti was a sage of rare qualities and characteristics. He was thus quite different in many respects from other sages and holy men of the twentieth century, who were out to liberate humanity from misery and ignorance through their techniques and practices. It would be very interesting and informative to go through these special qualities of J. Krishnamurti.

1. A large group of devoted followers had gathered around him from all over the world and the huge organisation had a lot of property with land, buildings, and funds for the work of the world teacher. But J. Krishnamurti renounced the whole gamut of tremendous wealth, power, authority and influence at his command, when he was thirty-four years of age and chose for himself the life of a 'nobody' for the rest of his life. In his entire life, he never charged any fees or gathered wealth. He was never forsaken, overlooked, ignored or neglected. His talks and discussions attracted a fairly large audience. He was always respected even by members of the Theosophical Society in spite of his revolt against their beliefs and programmes. That was because an inner change, a total revolution, had certainly taken place in him and his whole life and outlook had undergone a transformation. He had no vested interest in any activity. He had no craving left in his mind for fame, position, recognition or appreciation. Hence, he never repented his decision to renounce the position of world teacher. Anyone else in his place, if he had not undergone an inner change, would have continued to co-operate with Theosophy and enjoyed the position of the saviour, the messiah. But that position had no attraction for Krishnamurti because of the understanding that he had come to have from self-knowing. That was the rarest of the rare happening which had come about in his life and, subsequently, his whole life was associated with an exposition of that happening, for which

he used words like innocence, simplicity, austerity, discovery, freedom, benediction, bliss, humility, intelligence, and so on. Thus, 'a total inner revolution' was the first quality of J. Krishnamurti.

2. J. Krishnamurti cannot be called a man of the masses. He appealed to a very small proportion of people belonging to various countries. His admirers formed a very small section of society. The main reason for very few persons knowing about the sage was that he never raised false hopes or made extravagant claims in his talks. He had no vested interest in spreading his influence, in bringing people to his fold, in becoming famous, in acquiring money, followers, admirers, and so on. On the contrary, his contention was that everyone should look at oneself directly to know what one actually is, without any presuppositions, conclusions, and without any idea of 'what should be'. This has been a wholly new phenomenon, not explained by anyone before Krishnamurti. We are accustomed to be told what to do, and how to do it, in order to attain the ultimate truth, **ātman**, **brahman**, and so on.

   But Krishnamurti did not speak about any ultimate truth, any permanent goal or ideal, any method, any 'how', any way. That was always very perplexing for most people. His insistence was always on 'an inner change in oneself first' before thinking of reforming others. So he did not give any importance to social service, village uplift, and other such programmes of social work. He was never intimately related or involved with any Government institution, group of workers, society, association, or any socio-cultural organisation. He was engaged solely in just two activities throughout his life: giving talks at different places throughout the world, and running schools, one in the USA, one in England, and two in India. It was a fond belief entertained by J. Krishnamurti that proper facilities of right education would help to bring about an inner change in man, giving rise to a flowering of the personality, which could make for transformation, regeneration or mutation, resulting in integrally intelligent human beings.

Apart from this dual activity, he was almost cut off from society, although many people would visit him at his residence and discuss their problems of daily life with him. In a way, he was an ivory-tower man. His personal life was somewhat like that of a ruler of a princely state of British India, his whole life like an extended vacation. He was never decorated by any Government with awards, prizes or titles. Nor had there been any felicitation on the occasion of his 60th, 75th, or 81st birthdays. He never cared for any honour or felicitation. Indeed, he was very much a **Jivanmukta** or **Paramahamsa**—a man outwardly appearing 'ordinary' but inwardly enjoying freedom and bliss, silence and benediction. After his death, his funeral was attended by less than half a dozen persons, and he was cremated without any ceremony or ritual. Was all this not peculiar, remarkable and wholly different?

It appears that Krishnamurti was averse to any work for charity, helping the poor, downtrodden, and so on. Instead, he gave sole importance to transformation, regeneration, mutation, or total inner change of man. This may be clear from an account given by Pupul Jaykar as follows (3 : 283-284):

"In October 1963, Krishnamurti went to Rajghat. Achut told him he liked Vinoba's *bhoodan* work. (Achut was the great freedom fighter, Achutrao Patwardhan. His elder brother was Raosaheb Patwardhan). Work for the poor and oppressed could not be separated from religious life. Krishnamurti's response shook Achut deeply. Krishnamurti said, 'After all these years how can you be such an ass? Why are you fooling around? Look, my boy, if you were not to have met me, you would be in *sarvodaya*, cleaning the bottoms of village children. You are not in Rajghat to do that. You are self-righteously trying to change society. But deep change must start with man.'

"Achut was disappointed. He took six months off and went to the Himalayas. He returned in 1964 and discussed his conflict with Krishnamurti again. Krishnamurti said, 'Nothing has happened to you in Rajghat. So you should go. Rajghat is not helping you to flower.'

"Achut left Rajghat without bitterness. He went into retreat in Bangalore. Raosaheb was very upset. He felt hurt and developed high blood pressure and heart disease. Krishnamurti said that he had been speaking in India for thirty years and nothing had happened. 'There is not one person who is living the teaching.'"

This account shows how the sage considered 'radical transformation of man' as the only possible answer to all problems of human life, and that all other efforts involving reform, service, sacrifice were inadequate and misdirected.

3. It may appear very strange and unbelievable; yet it is a fact, a sad one, that although Krishnamurti began his independent career after severing relations with Theosophy in 1929 with the avowed concern to 'set man absolutely, unconditionally free' as mentioned by Mary Cadogan (2 : 1), this mission was never fulfilled in his lifetime. Indeed, till his death in 1986, there had been nobody who was set free by his teachings. This fact is not a piece of guesswork. It was said by Krishnamurti himself as mentioned by Pupul Jaykar (3 : 287) and Mary Lutyens (22 : 191). We have already given Pupul Jaykar's account above.

4. Spontaneity and directness of approach were two other special features of the life and teachings of J. Krishnamurti. He was not a man of plans, programmes, schemes, methods, and patterns of behaviour and thoughts. He never associated himself with any organisation or movement. His talks always used to be simple, direct and spontaneous. They were not preplanned regarding the subject matter. There was no particular arrangement of the material which he would like to convey to his audiences. He was not concerned about producing this or that result or any particular belief regarding life and the problems associated with it in the minds of his listeners. He never projected any goal or ideal, any path or system or any pattern of activity to be followed by those who attended his talks and discussions. Human life as we

live it and the human mind as we use it in our life were the two main aspects of his inquiry. He always dealt directly with a problem of human life or human behaviour. It was always a direct interaction, a communication, a going into the problem together, between the speaker and the audience. His attitude was always to explore, to share, to find out, to understand together, without one following the other.

Krishnamurti never spoke as a Hindu, or as a Brahmin, or a representative of any class, sect, community, or religion. He discussed various matters from the standpoint of every human being without any distinctions of caste, creed, language or group, never according to any particular tradition, conclusion or opinion.

As we shall see in the next chapter, the subject matter touched upon in his talks throughout his life can be said to consist of twelve main themes, each represented by an aphorism of the sage. We may call them the twelve main aphorisms of J. Krishnamurti, or the twelve great sayings, or **mahāvākyas**, or **āryasatyas**, or the twelve commandments of J. Krishnamurti. These aphorisms or great sayings were further associated with 187 different problems of human life. His talks related to any one or more of these 187 problems at random. They did not have any particular order or arrangement. That was the expression of spontaneity associated with the mind of the sage. Thus, each talk proceeded and flowered in its own way from what may have been uppermost in the mind of the speaker at that time. Lack of any particular order often made it difficult for the audience to arrive at the systematic whole from the talk, or a series of talks, or a variety of thoughts, not necessarily connected with each other with any order or system or arrangement. Thus, the listener was often at a loss to make out any harmonious impact or well-knit whole from the exceedingly diffuse material in spite of the very good English and the rare kind of purity, serenity, and simplicity of the speaker.

5. Krishnamurti never quoted from or referred to what others had said, what the opinions or conclusions of scriptures,

saints, authorities, experts, masters, or gurus were. On the contrary, he asked every listener to keep away from what was said by others, and perceive directly without pre-formed opinions and conclusions. This was a very unique, special feature of the teachings of the sage. Observing, listening, without an observer, thinker, experiencer, watcher, may be said to be a very fundamental tenet of J. Krishnamurti's whole life activity. This essence, the hallmark of his teachings, certainly marks him off as a one-of-his-kind world teacher who was different from all the sages and holy men ever known to humanity.

6. In Indian philosophy, the Hindu religion, or the ancient Indian tradition, there are six fundamental beliefs accepted by all schools, except the **Chārvāka**. They are: (*i*) God as an object of worship, (*ii*) soul, **ātman** as an abiding spiritual entity, (*iii*) the **karma** doctrine, according to which every act produces good or bad fruits, which must be enjoyed in the present or future births and every enjoyment and suffering is the result of previous good or bad deeds, (*iv*) the cycle of rebirth, (*v*) basic ignorance (**avidyā**), **as an initial endowment of everyone of us, and** (*vi*) **liberation, emancipation (moksha** or **mukti**).

   None of these beliefs had a place in Krishnamurti's teachings. He never advocated any of these beliefs. He never discussed them in his talks and writings and never sought any support from them. This approach of the sage may be looked upon as peculiar, rather objectionable, so far as the convictions and inclinations of many traditional Indian people go. Most of us are traditionally brought up with an unshakable faith in God, the merciful, in the **ātman** as a permanent entity which is not destroyed with the body at death, and in the law of **karma**. We have a very firm belief in the highest ultimate state of emancipation (**moksha**). It may be seen that many of us, who have been listening devotedly and regularly to the sage for decades and who have come to admire him for what he had been saying, are still not ready to come out of the overwhelming influence on their mind of the compelling faith in God, **ātman**, their guru, and the discipline and practice recommended by him in the spiritual domain. This was a very peculiar kind of relationship between J. Krishnamurti and his half-blind, half-devoted admirers. We like him very intensely, we have very high regard for him, yet we are still caught up in the net of our past, the conditioning caused by what we have been told by authorities accepted by us, our self-made prison. We are never free to die to the past, to have a young, fresh mind, uninfluenced by extraneous ideas and beliefs. Surely, Krishnamurti was completely helpless and inconsequential in bringing about any inner change in us, the common people, through his talks and writings.

There are two other special features which have been mentioned by Krishnamurti himself on several occasions. One of them is about himself, the other about his teachings. We shall go into them at some length, because they belong to Krishnamurti alone, and not to any other holy man. We need to be very clear in our mind about the importance and special significance of both of them.

7. **The speaker is not important:** Those who come to achieve fame and popularity in the spiritual field and are accepted by a large number of spirited and active followers as their guru, their only hope in despair, their pathfinder, their ideal to be emulated, and so on, start pretending to be endowed with supernatural powers, a superior intellect, and perfect understanding of human problems and their solutions. They consider themselves to be engaged in some divine work, at the command of the divine being, and to emphasise the existence of this divine touch, this divine commandment, they start using words like **'sri-sri'**, **'ananta-sri'**, **'muni-sri'**, **'maharishi'**, **'avatāra'**, **'Bhagavān'**, **'His holiness'** and so on, before their names. Their devotees and followers are strictly expected to use these words before their names and it is considered 'bad manners' not to associate such words with their names. Words like **'mahārāja'**, **'swāmi'**, **'muni'** are also quite commonly used after their names.

J. Krishnamurti was remarkably free from any such relationship with the divine. He would request his audience not to take the speaker as important in any way, or to follow him as an ideal, an authority, or to accept out of devotion, attachment, reverence, or the like, what he said, discussed and explained.

We must mention here a very fundamental difference between J. Krishnamurti on the one hand and all the other so-called holy men and gurus of the twentieth century, on the other. In spite of having undergone a very carefully drawn-out programme for twenty years to prepare him to look, speak, and behave like a world teacher, a saviour, a master of Theosophy, no vestige of that training, that preparation, was left in him after he renounced that position in 1929. He did not grow a beard, nor did he wield long black hair on the head. His dress was simple, like that of a common man. He never needed a cloak or a robe for exhibiting a divine connection, nor did things like ashes, rosaries and beads form part of his accessories. These extraneous appendages which have an extraordinary importance in the appearance, the make-up, and the manners and lifestyle of many **swāmis**, **maharishis**, and spiritual bigwigs of our times, had no meaning at all for J. Krishnamurti. His only 'make-up' consisted of wearing an Indian dress while in India, and a western dress in Europe and America. A rather unusual habit, which he had developed to conceal his baldness, was the peculiar style of growing and combing his hair from the sides in the forward direction, so as to cover the hairless part of the frontal region of the scalp. Perhaps there is only one photograph of the sage showing his baldness prominently. That was taken on his last walk on the Adyar beach, along with Mrs Radha Bernier, the President of the Theosophical Society. In it his hair are flowing backward due to strong winds, exposing the loss of hair on the anterior scalp. But it must be remembered that unlike other gurus and **swāmis**, J. Krishnamurti never took recourse to any facade, presenting an appearance with nothing substantial behind it.

8. **The teachings to be used as a mirror:** Krishnamurti would request his audience to observe and understand what he said without comparing it with what they already knew, or

without judging or examining it against the background of knowledge or beliefs. Instead, he implored us to look at it just as we see our face in a mirror. From what he said, from what was discussed and explained in the talk, one was requested to look at oneself, at one's own behaviour in life. It would be better to quote his own statements regarding the speaker not being important and the teaching being like a mirror, in order to make these two very important points clear.

"The speaker is merely a mirror and, therefore, what you see is yourself in the mirror. So the speaker is in no way important. What is important is what you see in the mirror. And to see clearly, precisely, without any distortion, every form of image must go—the image that you are an American or a Catholic, that you are a rich man or a poor man, all your prejudices must go. What we are concerned with is whether man, as he is, can radically bring about a transformation in himself... by seeing actually what he is." (6 : 15).

"Please do listen to this carefully. The speaker is not in the least important, but it is very important for you to understand the truth of what is being said." (24 : 135-136).

"Do please observe what I am talking about, not merely hear the words of the speaker, but observe yourselves, using the speaker as a mirror in which you can see yourselves. What the speaker has to say is of very little importance, and the speaker himself is of no importance whatsoever, but what you gather out of observing yourself is important. It is so because there must be a total revolution, a complete mutation in our minds, in our way of living, in our feelings, in the activities of our daily life." (14 : 188).

"Use the speaker as a mirror in which you see yourself now. What the speaker is saying is merely exposing yourself to yourself. And, therefore, look at this, listen to it and become completely in contact with it, be totally with it, and, if you are, you will see that there is immediate action." (14 : 214).

In spite of being urged again and again by the sage that we should not consider the speaker to be important and that we should take the teachings to be like a mirror in which to see ourselves as we are, our habit of thinking always prevents us from abiding by the two implorations of the sage as mentioned in the above statements. We just cannot stop or avoid taking him to be important, very important, for our spiritual well-being. We very much expect to be told what we should do and how to do it. We want him to show us a path, a way leading to the goal of ultimate truth or reality, which is a distant goal, hard to be realised or achieved. We are very inclined to take him to be holy, sacred, having a divine touch and commandment, and whatever he says to be sacrosanct, to be absorbed and retained with utmost care, with devotion. Most of us are, by our very habit, like that. We have other gurus and ideals also. We cannot help it. While hearing what he says, we compare it with what we already believe strongly or hazily. We accept or reject, appreciate or condemn while we hear Krishnamurti. Thus, our attention is divided, fragmented. We do not apply our mind totally to what is being said. Yet, that is what Krishnamurti requires all of us, his listeners, to do—give total attention. He has explained it very clearly in the following passage:

"What the speaker is saying may be utterly stupid and nonsensical, or it may be true. But to accept or to deny makes you remain as you are, dull, heavy, habit-ridden, insensitive. But in what we are going to say in a moment and even now, do not accept or compare with what you already know or what you have been told or read, but listen in order to find out for yourself what is true. And to give attention, to listen, you have to give your total attention. You cannot give your total attention if you are merely learning to concentrate, or if you are trying to concentrate on a few words, or on the meaning of words or what you have already heard. But give your attention, and this means listening without any barrier, without any interference or comparison, or condemnation; that is giving total attention; then you will find out for yourself what is true or false without being told. But this is one of the most difficult things to do—to give attention." (14 : 209).

In this statement, Krishnamurti has explained the fact that he expects everyone of us to find out for ourselves what is true or false without being told. And he has himself pointed out that this is one of the most difficult things to do.

This statement of the sage contains the reason why there were very few who could retain their interest in his teachings for long, and why there was none who could benefit adequately from his teachings.

— — —

## Chapter 2

# What Were the Teachings?

To the question 'what precisely are the teachings' or the main thrust of it, or the broad outline, the gist, the essential outlook, or the main features, a straight and exact answer was probably never given by the sage himself. As mentioned earlier, his whole life and teachings were marked by simplicity, directness and spontaneity. Nearly a quarter century after his death, no one who had come in contact with the sage for quite some time, and had a chance to speak to him personally about matters which were so dear to him regarding his avowed concern, that is to say, 'setting man free, absolutely, unconditionally'—no such person, man or woman, has come forward to discuss the crucial problem as to what precisely were the teachings of J. Krishnamurti, the greatest among great human beings that lived on earth during the twentieth century. Another quarter century later, there will probably be no one alive who might have had a chance to talk to the sage personally.

Just as we have the great sayings of the Upanishads called '**mahāvākyas**' or '**āryasatyas**' such as 'I am the ultimate reality of brahman' (**aham brahmāsmi**), 'You are that' (**tattvamasi**), 'The soul is brahman' (**ayamātmā brahma**), or we have the principle sayings of the Bhagavad Gita such as 'Yoga is skilful action' **(yogah karmasu kaushalam)**, or 'Equanimity is called yoga' **(samattvam yoga uchchate)**, similarly, it is possible to come upon some basic principles or fundamental truths or enunciatory utterances of the sage which form the very core, the essence, the substantial part of his teachings. I have found twelve such great sayings, **mahāvākyas**, **āryasatyas**, or twelve commandments of J. Krishnamurti. It is true that the sage himself never called them so. But they were, nevertheless, his own sayings, never called them so. But they were, nevertheless, his own sayings, what he had actually said, and obviously he said those words for us to understand, for our total attention. I have understood them as forming the very foundation on which his whole teachings may be said to stand. Any exposition of the teachings of J. Krishnamurti will have to include these fundamental tenets. In this second chapter 'What Were the Teachings', I shall discuss these twelve great sayings of J. Krishnamurti at some length. Perhaps such a thing is being done for the very first time by anyone interested in understanding the teachings of the sage, in his own words. I would give here the twelve great sayings first, and then each of them would be discussed separately. The twelve **mahāvākyas** of J. Krishnamurti are as follows:

1. There must be a radical revolution. The world crisis demands it. Our lives demand it. (16 : 262).
2. Self-knowledge is the beginning of wisdom and, therefore, the beginning of transformation or regeneration. (16 : 31).
3. Seeing is acting. (21 : 28).
4. Knowledge is a hindrance to understanding. (26 : 209).
5. Truth is not in some far distant place; it is the looking at '**what is**'. (25 : 37-38).
6. Negation is the most positive action. (25 : 200).
7. It is only when the mind is silent that there is a possibility of clarity. (21 : 106).
8. Only to the alone is there bliss. (26 : 158).
9. Freedom is always at the beginning and not at the end. (24 : 50).
10. Enlightenment does not come through another. It comes through your own observation, your own understanding of yourself. (6 : 137).
11. Craving for the permanent creates the permanent. (28 : 18).
12. Thought creates the thinker. (26 : 158).

## Mahāvākya No. 1

**There must be a radical revolution. The world crisis demands it. Our lives demand it.** (16 : 262).

J. Krishnamurti may not be regarded as a highly educated intellectual or an erudite scholar. He was not at all a well-read person so far as the scriptures were concerned. But he was an observer par excellence, having a sensitive, alert, fresh, new mind—a quality which, to be sure, is absent in many a writer, philosopher, orator, and reformer. He often spoke about innocence, austerity, humility, sensitivity, total attention, freedom, passion, and certainly he was himself the best possible example of a man having those qualities in him. He was the supreme artist of seeing, looking and listening. He described the importance of all these qualities tirelessly in his talks and writings. He must have observed very keenly and intimately human life, human mind, human relationship and human behaviour during the period when he was a world teacher, especially at the time of turmoil and great challenge thrown at him by the whole gamut of Theosophy, more so, after the death of his beloved brother Nityananda. In his observation of life in a state of deep silence and stillness, Krishnamurti must have come to understand very clearly the fact that the crisis the human world was going through for ages needed a radical revolution, a total transformation, a fundamental inner change, which could never come about through a slow, step-by-step process, according to a set pattern or idea, but only with an absolute suddenness. And this became the very first great saying he offered to humanity.

As we shall see presently from his own words, we are all living in a corrupt, rotten society. Our daily life is full of conflict, strife, confusion, suffering, exploitation, self-deception, violence, and war. Our scriptures, religious and spiritual leaders, politicians and reformers, all seem to agree that the present situation of disharmony, disorder and distrust must be brought to an end. It is looked upon by all of us as an extremely serious and urgent matter needing very careful attention, immediately. Religious, social, political reforms are advocated vehemently. Religion, philosophy, the law-enforcing organisation, political parties,

Government, and the law-making bodies and institutions are all engaged in improving the appalling situation we are in throughout the world. Krishnamurti observed these efforts towards reforming society to be like starting at the wrong end. Such reforms, as he has argued, lead to an endless process in which every reform stands in need of a further reform. Any such revolution arising out of an idea, a pattern or a foregone conclusion, as is seen in the efforts undertaken by religious, social and political organisations is, as observed by Krishnamurti, a wasteful, misdirected and inadequate activity, leading us nowhere. He emphasised that such activity has actually resulted in antagonism, ill-will, division, violence and war. Human suffering has not stopped at all by these efforts to change society through set patterns, coercion, and compulsion. The only answer to the modern human predicament, as explained by the sage, is through a total, fundamental change in man, not in society as a whole.

We shall, at this stage, quote a few statements of the sage.

"Obviously, there must be a radical revolution. The world crisis demands it. Our lives demand it.... There must be fundamental, radical revolution, because everything about us has collapsed. Though seemingly there is order, in fact there is slow decay, destruction: the wave of destruction is constantly overtaking the wave of life. So there must be a revolution—but not a revolution based on an idea. Such a revolution is merely a continuation of the idea, not a radical transformation. A revolution based on an idea brings bloodshed, disruption, chaos." (16 : 262).

"Seeing the whole of this catastrophe—the constant repetition of wars, the ceaseless conflict between classes, between peoples, the awful economic and social inequality, the inequality of capacity and gifts, the gulf between those who are extraordinarily happy, unruffled, and those who are caught in hate, conflict and misery—seeing all this there must be a revolution, there must be complete transformation." (16 : 262).

Krishnamurti has further clarified the fact that this transformation cannot be an ultimate thing, to be achieved in future. He has said, "It can only be 'now', from moment to moment." (16 : 263).

"What does transformation actually mean?" it may be asked. The answer of the sage to this question is as follows:

"Seeing the false as the false and the true as the true is transformation, because when you see something very clearly as the truth, that truth liberates. When you see that something is false, the false thing drops away.... As we are surrounded by so much that is false, perceiving the falseness from moment to moment is transformation. Truth is not cumulative. It is from moment to moment." (16 : 262).

This passage consists of one of the most fundamental observations concerning human life mentioned by J. Krishnamurti. It should be understood clearly, not merely literally. 'Seeing something very clearly' is a very crucial happening in Krishnamurti's teaching. It can happen in two very different ways. One way is like a smoker seeing the fact very clearly that smoking is injurious to health. That does not help him to get rid of the habit of smoking. What Krishnamurti means here by 'seeing something very clearly' is not this sort of seeing. The other way of seeing clearly is like perceiving the fact that fire burns, or a cobra is deadly. If one really perceives this fact, he would never touch fire or ignore a cobra. This seeing does liberate; it does mean appropriate action. Krishnamurti has used the words 'seeing clearly' here in this second sense. If we can see clearly the false as the false in this sense, then there is transformation.

A question may arise in our minds here, namely, how does transformation come about? What should we do actually for it to take place? Krishnamurti has explained this in the following words:

"To realise transformation, one must examine very closely what our life is, not escape from it, not indulge in theoretical beliefs and assertions, but observe very closely what our life actually is, and see whether it is possible to transform it completely. In the transformation of it you may affect the nature and the culture of society. There must be change in society, because there are so many evils and social injustices, there is an appalling travesty of worship and so on. But the change in society is of secondary importance; that will come about naturally, inevitably when you as a human being in relationship with another, bring about this change in yourself." (6 : 35-36).

Krishnamurti himself never took part in any cultural, social, reformatory work, or work of charity conducted by any organisastion, trust, society or association. He was convinced about the primary importance of bringing about a change in oneself before trying to change others, or to help others socially, culturally, or economically. It was due to this that he rebuked Achutrao Patwardhan as mentioned by us earlier, when he expressed a wish to join the *bhoodan* movement of Acharya Vinoba Bhave. This point is further clarified by the sage in the following statements:

"It is we ourselves that have to change, not society. Do please realise this. We have to bring about in ourselves, at the highest and at the deepest levels, a change in our whole way of thinking, living, feeling; then only is the social change possible.... To bring about such a change in ourselves is a lifetime's work.... It is a constant application, a constant awareness of what is going on, within and without." (6 : 163-164).

About the need for change in ourselves, here is another important statement of the sage. (14 : 59-60).

"One sees that there must be change in oneself—the more sensitive, the more alert and intelligent one is, the more one is aware that there must be a deep, abiding, living change. ...One needs a great deal of passion, great energy, and most of us waste our energies in conflict."

About the man who undergoes a deep inner change, the sage has pointed out the following facts:

"A man who is passionate about the world and the necessity for change, must be free from political activity, religious *conformity* and tradition—which means, free from the weight of time, free from the burden of the past, free from all the action of will: this is the new human being. This only is the social, psychological, and even the political revolution." (25 : 318).

There are three more important statements of the sage regarding transformation, regeneration, revolution or mutation. They are reproduced below:

"There must be a total revolution, a complete mutation in our minds, in our way of living, in our feeling, in the activities of our daily life. And to bring about such fundamental, deep revolution is only possible when we know how to look." (14 : 188-189).

"Revolution is only possible **now**, not in the future; regeneration is today, not tomorrow. ...When the mind is still, tranquil, not seeking—it is only then that there can be a regeneration, because then the mind is capable of perceiving what is true." (24 : 89-90).

"We need great intelligence to live, to live our daily life, because it is only intelligence that can possibly bring about a total revolution in our psyche, in the very core of our being. And such a mutation is necessary, because man has lived for millions of years in agony, in despair, always battling with himself and with the world." (14 : 210).

## Mahāvākya No. 2

**Self-knowledge is the beginning of wisdom, and therefore the beginning of transformation or regeneration.** (16 : 31).

Self-knowledge is one of the most important and oft-repeated key words in Krishnamurti's teachings. It has been used for many centuries by Indian philosophers and thinkers with great reverence. There are many Sanskrit equivalents of it, like **ātmajnyāna**, **ātmasākshātkāra**, **ātmadarshana, ātmānubhūti**, **aparokshānubhūti**, and so on. There is a vast difference between the meaning of the word 'self-knowledge' as used by the sage, and the meaning of the Sanskrit words mentioned here, which are all its synonyms. Our ancients believed in the existence of an abiding soul (the **ātman**) which went through a cycle of rebirths. The knowledge of it being a permanent, indestructible spiritual being was what they called self-knowledge. This spiritual knowledge was understood to be direct knowledge, which was different from the knowledge of the world and its objects, derived from sense experience (**pratyaksha**), inference (**anumāna**) and testimony or authority (**āgama**). It was called absolute knowledge (**pāramārthikajnyāna**).

J. Krishnamurti did not entertain any belief in the soul (**ātman**) as a transcendental spiritual reality. By 'self' in self-knowledge, he understood 'what we actually are', and not 'what we wish to be', or 'what we think we are'. 'Self-knowledge', according to him, means our understanding of ourselves by direct perception as we behave in daily life, in our relationship with persons, things or events and ideas. We know ourselves directly in the mirror of relationship with our surroundings. Knowing directly means knowing by observing without the interference of past knowledge, what is told by others, what is written in the scriptures, and what is taught by saints, etc. The knowledge of what we actually are is the beginning of wisdom. It was pointed out by the sage that self-knowledge brings about transformation or regeneration, as explained in the first **mahāvākya**.

Let us go through some of his statements wherein he has explained the state of self-knowledge.

"It seems to me that before we set out on a journey to find reality, to find God, before we can act, before we can have any relationship with another, which is society, it is essential that we begin to understand ourselves." (24 : 12).

This statement contains a truth of which we are usually never aware. Without knowing ourselves first we accept what we are taught, what we are told, and we set out on a journey on that basis, taking that for granted. That becomes our conditioning, our 'known', our past, our veil or screen, through which we always look at the world and at ourselves. And we are hardly ever aware of this fact. The burden of the past prevents us from looking directly at anything. We always look through this burden, this conditioning. The sage has said:

"The problems of the world are so colossal, so very complex, that to understand, and so to resolve them one must approach them in a very simple and direct manner; and simplicity, directness, do not depend on outward circumstances, nor on our particular prejudices and moods. ...The solution is not to be found through conferences, blueprints, or through the substitution of new leaders for the old and so on. The solution obviously lies in the creator of that problem, of the hate and the enormous misunderstanding that exists between human beings. The creator of this mischief, the creator of these problems is the individual, you and I, not the world as we think of it. The world is your relationship with another. The world is not something separate from you and me; the world, society, is the relationship that we establish or seek to establish between each other." (16 : 30).

How can we know ourselves? This problem is explained in the following statements:

"To know ourselves means to know our relationship with the world—not only with the world of ideas and people, but also with nature, with the things we possess." (24 : 67).

"I can observe myself only in relationship, because all life is relationship. It is no use sitting in a corner meditating about myself. I exist only in relationship to people, things and ideas, and in studying my relationship to outward things and people as well as to inward things, I begin to understand myself. Every other form of understanding is merely an abstraction. I have to study myself as I am, not as I wish to be." (21 : 22).

It is clear from these passages that it is essential to understand the fact that self-knowledge is not knowing oneself according to what is said in the scriptures, our religious tradition, or by this or that authority. Self-knowledge needs the understanding of the relationship between ourselves and the inner and outer world. We must observe how we behave, how we think, how almost all of our thinking is wishful thinking, and how we lack the intention to understand ourselves as we are. Observing with total, undistracted attention is necessary.

## Mahāvākya No. 3

**Seeing is acting.** (21 : 28).

This is one of the most remarkable findings of J. Krishnamurti. This is one of those statements which appear to be simple but are actually difficult to grasp. It is the experience of all of us that 'seeing' and 'acting' are very different from each other. Seeing involves sensory impulses, while acting is brought about by motor impulses. Both may be simultaneous. Acting many a time depends on seeing.

When Krishnamurti says 'seeing is acting', the word 'seeing' is used by him in a very special sense. In daily life, when we see something, the whole store of the traces of past experience in our brain cells takes part in that seeing, and we understand, interpret, and react to what is seen on the basis of this store of past experiences. Our memories, knowledge, likes and dislikes, conclusions, cravings, all influence our response to what we see. Thus, the whole content of our consciousness is always taking part in the process of seeing. Our seeing is associated continuously with a process of distraction, dissipation of energy, resulting in attention that is not complete, total, but partial, limited, divided. By 'seeing', Krishnamurti means the act of observing, looking, understanding, without memory and thought taking any part in it. It means total attention, direct perception, without condemning, judging, naming, or justifying. When there is seeing anything in this way, there is immediate, spontaneous action. Krishnamurti has explained the important fact that seeing like this even for a second in deep silence is enough. The importance of a still mind is very great for that seeing to take place. Here are two original statements of the sage explaining this point:

"To see temporarily is sufficient. If you can see it for a fleeting second, it is enough, because you will then see an extraordinary thing taking place. The unconscious is at work, though the conscious may reject. It is not a progressive second; but that second is the only thing, and it will have its own results, even in spite of the conscious mind struggling against it." (24 : 41).

"A still mind is possible only when the brain itself is quiet. The brain cells which have been conditioned for so long to react, to project, to depend, to assert, become quiet only through the seeing of what actually is. From this silence, action which does not bring about disorder is possible only when the observer, the centre, the experiencer, has come to an end—for then the seeing is doing. Seeing is possible only out of a silence in which all evaluative and moral values have come to an end." (25 : 51).

Stillness of the mind, which must be there for seeing to take place, is a state we do not experience. We do not have a silent mind because we are always under the influence of the ‘me’, the ‘self’, which is an imaginary entity, an image we form of ourselves from memories, thoughts, cravings, beliefs, emotions, and so on. This is an extremely crucial point, a fact brought out by the sage again and again in his discourses.

Here is another important aspect of seeing as explained by the sage:

“Seeing is one thing and seeing something is another. ...Seeing through knowledge, the object, the image, the symbol, and seeing—these are entirely different.” (19 : 144).

In this statement the sage has differentiated between ‘total seeing’, which means ‘seeing **what is**’ and seeing based on one’s own knowledge. The former always brings about spontaneous action. This ‘total seeing’ is described by the sage thus:

“The brain has to be in a state of negation for total seeing; it must not interfere with its evaluations and justifications, with its condemnations and defences. It has to be still, not **made** still by compulsion of any kind, for then it is a dead brain, merely imitating and conforming. When it is in a state of negation, it is choicelessly still. Only then is there total seeing. In this total seeing which is a quality of the mind, there is no seer, no observer, no experiencer, there is only seeing. The mind is then completely awake. In this fully awakened state, there is no observer and the observed; there is only light, clarity. The contradiction and conflict between the thinker and thought ceases.” (10 : 126).

The concept of the observer and the observed, which is one that must be understood carefully by everyone of us, will be explained later.

## Mahāvākya No. 4

**Knowledge is a hindrance to understanding.** (26 : 209).

In the Bhagavad Gita (IV : 38) Lord Krishna has declared that in this world there is nothing as sacred as knowledge and that the devoted yoga aspirant attains knowledge which liberates after a long time. The importance of knowledge for success in daily life is beyond any dispute. Everyone recognises it without any doubt. So the above statement of the sage comes to many of us as something most unbelievable. But actually it is not so. This is not the only saying of the sage that we receive with shock and disbelief. There are at least half a dozen other statements which cause this same reaction in our minds. Actually, all of them are **mahāvākyas**. The only difficulty with most of us is that these truths need to be explained to us clearly in familiar terms. This task has never been undertaken by anyone in the lifetime of the sage. This book is aimed at fulfilling that unfinished task.

The importance of knowledge in daily life is quite evident. Knowing a language, remembering facts and events, the ability to use various techniques and skills, the capacity to communicate etc. are all examples of knowledge. Krishnamurti never objected to these forms of knowledge. His objection was to their utility for understanding **'what is'**. Self-knowledge or awakening of intelligence does not come about from that sort of knowledge. This was a finding of special importance in Krishnamurti's teachings. Knowledge is not a hindrance in daily life, in going to the office, coming home, talking with friends and relatives, and doing one's job. But it is certainly a hindrance in understanding ourselves. The statements of the sage explaining this fact are given below:

"While knowledge is necessary at one level, at another level it becomes a hindrance. There is a great deal of knowledge available about physical existence, and it is being added to all the time. It is essential to have such knowledge and to utilise it for the benefit of man. But is there not another kind of knowledge which, at the psychological level, becomes a hindrance to the discovery of what is true? After all, knowledge is a kind of tradition, is it not? And tradition is the cultivation of memory. Tradition in mechanical affairs is essential, but when tradition is used as a means of guiding man inwardly, it becomes a hindrance to the discovery of great things." (24 : 146).

"Knowledge is essential to technique, as coal to the engine, but it cannot reach out into the unknown. The unknown is not to be caught in the net of the known. Knowledge must be set aside for the unknown to be: but how difficult that is." (26 : 26).

This important point is clarified in another way, thus:

"The gathering of facts does not make for the understanding of life. Knowledge is one thing, and understanding, another. Knowledge does not lead to understanding. ...Knowledge is essential and not to be despised. Without knowledge, modern surgery and a hundred other marvels could not exist." (28 : 3).

## Mahāvākya No. 5

**Truth is not in some far distant place; it is the looking at 'what is'.** (25 : 37-38).

The notion of truth plays an exceedingly important role in human life. In the life of animals, its significance is negligible, because they do not use language to describe events, happenings, and ideas. Truth is purely a linguistic notion. It can be relevant to only what is said or expressed in any language. Primarily, it is the many beliefs that we have, which are true or false. Having a true belief is very important in human life, because it leads to success, progress and achievements. A false belief results in failure, disappointment and misery. Many of our beliefs are false, not true. But initially they are held to be true and in course of time, their falsehood becomes clear and the need to modify or abandon them is felt. The idea of absolute or ultimate truth such as God, the **ātman**, **brahman**, and so on, is one such belief which has influenced humanity for a long time. It is a very strongly and very fondly held belief. Krishnamurti has treated this belief disparagingly. He does not look at truth as something permanent, unchanging and indestructible. He has explained that truth is ever new, from moment to moment, not of the past, not pre-determined. This view is very different from the traditional view about truth. Our habit of thinking makes it difficult to understand. The following statements of the sage would be useful to make his idea of truth clear:

"The human mind wants permanency in everything—in relationship, in property, in virtue. It wants something which cannot be destroyed. That is why we say God is permanent, or truth is absolute. ...Truth is to be discovered and understood in every action, in every thought, in every feeling, howsoever trivial or transient; it is to be observed at each moment of every day. ...Your thinking may be false, it may be conditioned, limited, and to discover that your thinking is conditioned, limited, is truth. That very discovery sets your mind free from limitation. If you discover that you are greedy—if you **discover** it, and are not just told by somebody else—that discovery is truth, and that truth has its own action upon your greed. Truth is not something which you can gather, accumulate, store up and then rely on as a guide. ...When you realise the significance of this, you will find out what an extraordinary thing truth is. Truth is timeless, but the moment you capture it—as and when you say, 'I have found truth, it is mine'—it is no longer truth." (24 : 192-193).

This rather lengthy statement explains clearly what the sage meant by truth. It must be understood carefully by reading it again and again.

Krishnamurti has said another very significant fact about truth, which we would do well to understand properly. It is said in very few words:

"Truth is there, where you never look." (25 : 16).

Another important fact is said in the following statement:

"Truth is not to be comprehended through the passage of time. Truth is not a thing to be attained... it cannot be perceived gradually." (26 : 125).

Here is a statement of the sage containing another fact about truth:

"None of the agonies of suppression nor the brutal discipline of conforming to a pattern has led to truth. To come upon truth the mind must be completely free, without a spot of distortion." (21 : 67).

In the following statement the sage has explained how we can arrive at truth by understanding our prejudices:

"When you understand the nature of thought—not verbally, but are actually aware of it—then when you have prejudice, look at it and you will see that your religions are a prejudice, the identification with your country is a prejudice. We have so many opinions, so many prejudices; just observe one completely, with your heart, with your mind, with love—care for it, look at it. And then you will see how to live without any prejudice. It is only a mind that is free from prejudice, from conflict, that can see what truth is." (6 : 122).

## Mahāvākya No. 6

**Negation is the most positive action.** (25 : 200).

We include under positive action such programme or pattern of activity which would eventually lead to the attainment of a goal. It is an action which would yield a desired result. If one is neglectful, lacks proper attention and care, and fails to put in sufficient effort, that may be understood as negative action. J. Krishnamurti did not mean this by the word 'negation'. His **mahāvākya** is not to be applied to the events of daily life but to the affairs of religious and spiritual domains. Here also we are inclined to believe that for achieving the highest goal of emancipation or liberation (**mukti**) it is necessary to undergo rigorous spiritual effort, discipline, **sādhanā**, under the guidance of a guru, which is certainly a positive action. And this goal can only be achieved slowly, step by step, with determined progress on the spiritual path. If this belief is true, then what does Krishnamurti mean by negation as the most positive action? That is explained in the following statement of the sage:

"Negation is the most positive action, not positive assertion. This is a very important thing to understand. Most of us so easily accept positive dogma, a positive creed, because we want to be secure, to belong, to be attached, to depend. ...A positive statement in its very definition separates, and separation is resistance. To this we are accustomed, this is our conditioning. ...To negate everything that man has invented, to negate all his values, ethics and gods, is to be in a state of mind in which there is no duality, therefore no resistance or conflict between opposites. ...To deny all this is to deny oneself, and oneself is the conditioned entity. ...To most of us negation appears as a vacuum, because we know activity only in the prison of our conditioning, fear and misery. From that we look at negation and imagine it to be some terrible state of oblivion or emptiness. To the man who has negated all the assertions of society, culture, religion, and morality, the man who is still in the prison of social conformity is a man of sorrow. Negation is the state of enlightenment which functions in all the activities of a man who is free of the past. It is the past with the tradition and its authority that has to be negated. Negation is freedom, and it is the free man who lives, loves, and knows what it means to die." (7 : 32-33).

This is not an easy statement to understand. It contains many key words which are not defined or explained by the sage here. This book purports to explain the key words of J. Krishnamurti in order to help inquisitive persons to understand his sayings easily and clearly and to benefit from them more readily and effectively. It is hoped that after reading this book first, if one reads any book of J. Krishnamurti, it may be seen that the understanding of that book may be facilitated due to the explanations of the key words used by the sage provided in this book.

Here is another statement of the sage about the subject under discussion here, which is easier to understand:

"Negation can only take place when the mind sees the false. The very perception of the false is the negation of the false. And when you see the religions based on miracles, based on personal worship, based on fear that your own life is so shoddy, empty, meaningless, and that you are so transient, you will be gone in a few years, then the mind creates the image which is eternal, marvellous, beautiful, heaven and identifies with it and worships it. Because it deeply needs a sense of security, it has created all this superficial nonsense, this circus—it is a circus. So can the mind observe this phenomenon and see its own demand for security, comfort, safety, permanence, and deny all that? Deny in the sense of seeing how the brain, thought, creates the sense of permanency, the eternal, or whatever you like to call it." (1 : 212).

In this statement, Krishnamurti has brought out a most significant, extremely influential and fundamental dimension of human nature and human life. It is the basic tendency of all of us to demand security in life. Of course, security is an essential pre-requisite, a necessary condition for making not only human life alone but any kind of life possible at all. That security made by a congenial atmosphere is available only on planet earth in the solar system, and so life could make its appearance on this planet (which happened probably 1700 million years ago). The congeniality of atmosphere is made by a proper range of temperature, atmospheric pressure, availability of oxygen, water, life-sustaining food materials and absence of poisonous gases in the atmosphere, etc. This item of security has been available on earth.

The human mind, however, takes the demand for security rather too far, and it demands psychological security, which takes the form of a permanent, eternal, omnipotent being. This is the root cause of man's idea of **ātman**, **brahman**, God. Krishnamurti wants us all to understand very deeply, in a direct, straightforward manner, this fact of the process which has taken place in the minds of human beings alone, in the whole of the animal world. That is because man has come to have the ability to imagine, to think, to entertain abstract thinking, to form ideas. This capacity is the outcome of the development of particular areas of the human brain in the evolutionary process which has continued for the past few million years. To see the fact very clearly, directly, immediately, that our notion regarding God in different religions, traditions, and all that we do to obtain his grace, in order to be secure, is a product of the demand for security going out of hand, means to be free from that demand. That is negation. That is the most positive action. This truth has been made clear by no other sage except J. Krishnamurti. He alone has made us aware of it.

One very important fact about negation is that it is not an action produced as a result of thinking, opinion or conclusion. It is a natural outcome of seeing directly the falsity of a notion or belief. Hence, negation is the most positive action.

## Mahāvākya No. 7

**It is only when the mind is silent that there is a possibility of clarity.** (21 : 106).

The human mind is remarkably unsteady, almost completely lacking silence, quietitude, tranquillity and stillness. It has a very pronounced habit of constantly moving from thought to thought, object to object, desire to desire. The importance of a silent, steady mind is discussed since ancient times in all religions. In the Bhagavad Gita and in the Yogasūtra of Patanjali, the stages through which one can attain mental steadiness have been discussed in detail. The two principal means to this, as mentioned in the two texts (Gita-VI : 35; Yogasutra-I : 12) are : (*i*) concentration of mind (**abhyāsa**), and (*ii*) dispassionateness (**vairāgya**).

Krishnamurti has clearly distinguished between the mind that **is** silent, and the one that is **made** silent. There is a world of difference between the two, and the difference is very crucial. It is brought out by the sage in the two passages given below:

"Obviously, the mind can be made still by the repetition of a word, of a chant, of a prayer. The mind can be drugged, put to sleep. ...But the mind that is made quiet by discipline, by ritual, by repetition, can never be alert, sensitive and free." (26 : 84).

"If the mind is made still, then whatever comes into it is only a self-projection, the response of memory. With the understanding of its conditioning, with the choiceless awareness of its own responses as thought and feeling tranquillity comes to the mind." (27 : 81).

Natural tranquillity, which is brought about by understanding the working of the mind, and not by any discipline, effort to concentrate, is the state of mind which is essential for clarity. The importance of this kind of tranquillity is explained by the sage in the following words:

"It is only if you are aware of inward insufficiency and live with it without escape, accepting it wholly, that you will discover an extraordinary tranquillity, a tranquillity which is not put together, made up, but a tranquillity which comes with understanding of **what is**." (24 : 46).

One may be tempted to ask here how one can come to have such a tranquil, silent mind, if no effort, discipline, or concentration of mind is to be gone into. This is explained by the sage in two statements thus:

"This has been the problem of all religious people throughout the centuries; they realise that you must have a very quiet mind, because then only can you see. If you are chattering, if your mind is constantly in movement, rushing all over the place, obviously it cannot look, it cannot listen totally. ...Therefore they say control, hold on, and concentrate. When you do all that, you are in conflict and, therefore, there has to be more control, more subjugation. This has been going on for millennia, because they realise they must have a quiet mind. Now, how does the mind become quiet? Can the mind become quiet? ...How is it to happen? ...It is only such a mind that sees the whole of life as a unit, as a unitary movement, not fragmented. Therefore, such a mind acts totally, not fragmentarily, because it acts out of complete stillness." (14 : 97-98).

"If one wants to see a thing very clearly, one's mind must be very quiet, without all the prejudices, the chattering, the dialogue, the image, the picture—all that must be put aside to look. And it is only in silence that you can observe the beginning of thought—not when you are searching, asking questions, waiting for a reply." (21 : 103).

This point will be more clearly understood when it will be discussed more thoroughly later while considering meditation in the next chapter.

## Mahāvākya No. 8

**Only to the alone is there bliss.** (26 : 158).

'Alone' ordinarily means 'unaccompanied by anyone else or anything'. We come in this world alone (except in case of twins) and death is everyone's own, separate affair. Between these two points of the beginning and end of our life, we usually do not like to be alone. Krishnamurti has used the word alone in a very special sense. It is one of his most important key words. He calls one alone when one sets aside and is free from memories, ideas, notions, beliefs, opinions, conclusions, desires, cravings, pursuits and efforts to be or not to be something. He differentiates between aloneness and loneliness. In the latter state, there is a feeling of being overlooked, forlorn, forsaken, isolated, neglected, ignored and abandoned. It would be interesting to see how he describes the word 'alone'.

"We are never alone; we are surrounded by people and by our own thoughts. Even when the people are distant we see things through the screen of our thoughts. There is no moment, or it is very rare, when thought is not. We do not know what it is to be alone, to be free of all association, of all continuity, of all word and image. We are lonely, but we do not know what it is to be alone. The ache of loneliness fills our hearts, and the mind covers it with fear. Loneliness, that deep isolation, is the dark shadow of our life. We do everything we can to run away from it, we plunge down every avenue of escape we know, but it pursues us and we are never without it. Isolation is the way of our life. ...In ourselves we are not whole, complete. ...To walk alone, unimpeded by thought, by the trail of our desires, is to go beyond the reaches of the mind. It is the mind that isolates, separates, and cuts off communication. ...Aloneness is not the result of thought. Only when thought is utterly still is there the flight of the alone to the alone." (27 : 86-87).

"To deny is to be alone; alone from all influence, tradition, from need with its dependence and attachment. To be alone is to deny the conditioning, the background. ...To be choicelessly aware of this conditioning and the total denial of it is to be alone. This aloneness is not isolation, loneliness, self-enclosing occupation. Aloneness is not withdrawal from life. On the contrary, it is the total freedom from conflict and sorrow, from fear and death. This aloneness is the mutation of consciousness, complete transformation of what has been. This aloneness is emptiness. It is neither the positive state of being nor the not being. It is emptiness; in this fire of emptiness the mind is made young, fresh, and innocent." (10 : 111).

From these passages, it may be said that aloneness is the unity, a combination of all the key states of J. Krishnamurti's teachings, namely, negation, freedom, and transformation. This is a point worth noting and clearly understanding without any ambiguity. A question that would arise in our mind at this stage would be: why are we afraid of being alone? As an answer to this question, the sage has said:

"We want security, both outwardly and inwardly; therefore we depend on people, whether it is the priest, or the leader or the guru who says: 'I have experienced, that is why I know'. One has to stand completely alone—not isolated. There is a vast difference between isolation and being completely alone, integral. ...Aloneness implies a mind that does not depend on another psychologically, is not attached to a person." (14 : 93).

Another question connected with aloneness arising in our mind would be: why is bliss only to the alone? Krishnamurti has discussed this question in the following manner:

"Can a mind caught in endless becoming be aware of bliss? Can a mind that has imposed discipline upon itself ever be free to receive that bliss? Through effort and struggle, through resistance and denials, the mind makes itself insensitive. ...Through the desire for bliss have you not built a wall around yourself which the imponderable, the unknown, cannot penetrate. Have you not effectively shut yourself off from the new? Out of the old, you have made a path for the new; and can the new be contained in the old? ...In freedom alone is there discovery, sensitivity to receive. Without freedom there can be no bliss; but freedom does not come through discipline." (26 : 157).

The point to be noted very clearly in this discussion is that when one starts with a conclusion, a belief, a goal set by one's own illusory ideas, and begins to follow a guru or saint, one is really being led to a blind alley. One cannot be transformed that way. It is only when there is freedom from discipline, strife, path, supposedly leading to enlightenment, only when there is no dependence on another, is there the possibility of bliss. Hence it is said that 'only to the alone is there bliss'.

## Mahāvākya No. 9

**Freedom is always at the beginning and not at the end.** (24 : 50).

Freedom and bondage are words indicating two states which are exclusive of each other. Where there is bondage, freedom can't exist. Birds are free to fly, fishes are free to swim, and human beings are free to think, and most of us, the common people, are free, indeed very free, to think wrongly. The Indians were in bondage, but the British Parliament decided to make them a free nation and a dismembered nation, and they were granted 'freedom'.

When Krishnamurti says that 'freedom is always at the beginning', obviously, he is not attributing to the word 'freedom' the meaning of that word in the above sentences. What does he mean by freedom? It is 'freedom to see', to look, to listen, to observe, to understand **'what is'**, freedom to be 'integrally intelligent'. That freedom is denied to us, ever since we are born, until we breathe our last. What is it that denies freedom to us in Krishnamurti's special sense of that word? Our ancients argued that it was our own **karma**, traces of past deeds stored in our minds. **Karmāshaya**, they said, was the cause of our bondage. It binds us to the world of experience **(samsāra)** in an unbroken chain of rebirth. So freedom to our ancients meant freedom from the cycle of rebirth. That freedom could be obtained only at the **end** of a prolonged effort, never in the beginning. That freedom was called **'mukti'**, or **'moksha'**.

Krishnamurti's freedom can also be called **mukti** or **moksha** in Sanskrit. But it is not freedom from **samsāra**, but freedom from our own conditioning, the past, freedom from the known, the prison of ideas and images that we build around ourselves. The prison is of our own making. We make it out of our traditional beliefs, cultural entanglements, from what is said by our scriptures, saints, and holy men. Freedom from that prison of our own making can take place only by being passively aware of it, by looking at it directly, without any interference of knowledge and belief, prejudices and conclusions. That freedom to look must always be at the beginning, and not at the end. There is a very intimate relation between that freedom to look, and negation, stillness, self-knowledge, and transformation. This is a very crucial fact about the whole matter brought out by the sage. Let us see some of his original statements.

"Many people in this world are independent, but very few are free. ...To be free is to be intelligent, but intelligence does not come into being by just wishing to be free; it comes into being only when you begin to understand your whole environment, the social, religious, parental and traditional influences that are continually closing in on you. But to understand the various influences—the influence of your parents, of your Government, of society, of the culture to which you belong, of your beliefs, your gods, and superstitions, of the tradition to which you conform unthinkingly—to understand all these and become free from them requires deep insight; but you generally give in to them because inwardly you are frightened. ...But the man or the woman who sees the absurdity of all these things and whose heart is therefore innocent, and therefore not moved by the desire to be somebody—such a person is free. If you understand the simplicity of it you will also see its extraordinary beauty and depth." (24 : 112-113).

The fact of 'not being moved by the desire to be somebody' brought out here by the sage, may be pointed out as the very crux of the whole teachings of J. Krishnamurti. Usually we miss the importance of this fact completely, we never notice it in our life, because we are immersed in the flood of extraneous influences. The sage has done a really great job in bringing it so vividly to our notice. Here is another very significant statement of his.

"Freedom can only come about naturally, not through wishing, wanting, longing. Nor will you find it by creating an image of what you think it is. To come upon it, the mind has to learn to look at life, which is a vast movement, without the bondage of time, for freedom lies beyond the field of consciousness." (21 : 71).

Here is one more statement:

"To find out anything there must be freedom. To find out what I think, what I feel, what are my motives, to find out, not merely to analyse intellectually, but to find out, there must be freedom to look. ...To look, you must be free from knowledge; freedom is a quality of mind that cannot be got through renunciation, nor sacrifice. ...Freedom is a quality of mind that is essential for seeing. It is not freedom **from** something. If you are free **from** something, that is not freedom, it is only a reaction." (14 : 198-199).

## Mahāvākya No. 10

**Enlightenment does not come through another. It comes through your own observation, your own understanding of yourself.** (6 : 137).

Our ancients, whether they followed the tradition of Vedānta, Mimāmsā Nyāya, Vaisheshika, Sāmkhya or Yoga (which were called the orthodox schools), or the heretic tradition, that of Buddhism or Jainism, were all united in believing that basically, initially, we are all endowed with gross ignorance **(avidyā)** regarding our own true nature. To dispel this **avidyā**, it was considered most essential to have two things, namely, the guidance of a guru who is himself free from ignorance, and severe practise of discipline (**sādhanā**) which ultimately results in complete purification of the mind, the instrument of knowledge. To us, who have inherited this line of approach, the **mahāvākya** mentioned above comes as something most unbelievable. It would destroy the very basis of our whole culture, philosophy, tradition, and the veracity of our scriptures, gurus, and saints. Hence, it is very important to know exactly what Krishnamurti means by this **mahāvākya.**

One may naturally like to ask: Why can't enlightenment come through another? Enlightenment, understanding, wisdom is marked by the end of illusion, conditioning, self-deception. And that can only happen, as Krishnamurti has explained, by seeing the false as the false, by passive awareness or direct perception. Direct perception needs putting aside all that is already there in the mind, which means freedom from the known. And this is something which one has to understand and do for and by oneself. If I get up from a pleasant dream and start asking where the pleasant objects of enjoyment have gone, how they have disappeared, and I insist on others finding them for me, then nobody on earth can bring to me those objects. It is I alone who can see the false as the false and stop seeking, searching. This **mahāvākya** explains this very thing. Let us see Krishnamurti's own words about it:

"We are an odd people; we wander in search of something in far-off places when it is so close to us. ...We go to the other side of the world to find the Master. ...We do not know ourselves but we are willing to serve or follow him who promises a reward, a hope, a utopia. As long as we are confused, what we choose must also be confused. We cannot perceive clearly when we are half-blind; and what we see is only partial and so not real. We know all this, and yet our desires, our cravings are so strong that they drive us into illusions and endless miseries." (26 : 72-73).

"There is no intermediary between you and reality; and if there is one, he is a perverter, a mischief-maker. It does not matter **who** he is, whether the highest saviour or your latest guru or teacher. ...It is important to find out why you follow. You only follow to become something, to gain, to be clear. Clarity cannot be given by another. Confusion is in **us**. We have brought it about and we have to clear it away. ...The setting up of authority and the following of it is the denial of understanding. When there is understanding, there is freedom, which cannot be bought or given by another." (26 : 66-67).

## Mahāvākya No. 11

**Craving for the permanent creates the permanent.** (28 : 18).

The notion of a permanent entity like God, the soul, **brahman**, appears to play an exceedingly important role in every religion and its view of the universe. Why has this notion of a permanent being come to acquire such great importance and attraction for the human mind? This is an important question to ask ourselves. If such a notion of an eternal entity is shown to be intangible, unwarranted, unacceptable, that would be absolutely shocking to most of us. Krishnamurti, in the **mahāvākya** noted here, may have created such a shock in the minds of many of us. We should try to understand why he has said that the idea of permanence has as its source the craving for the permanent. His original statements are given below:

"You think there is a permanent soul, a permanent entity. Is there anything permanent in you? The moment you say there is a permanent soul, a permanent entity, that entity is the result of your thinking, or the result of your hopes, because there is so much insecurity, everything is transient, in a flux, in a movement. So when you say there is something permanent, that permanency is the result of your thinking. And thought is of the past, thought is never free—it can invent anything it likes." (14 : 82-83).

The fact is that most of our thinking is wishful thinking. Our wishes always act as a driving force underlying our thinking. The experience of impermanence, insecurity, decay and death is not liked by the human mind. The demand for security, permanence, continued existence is promoted, prompted, projected, by the experience of and the dislike for impermanence and insecurity. That causes the human mind to posit, to imagine, to believe that beyond this world, underlying this world, there is something which lasts forever, which is never destroyed. The mind accepts the idea of the imperishable, the indestructible, very readily, without doubting, without questioning, for it helps to remove the uneasiness caused by impermanence, insecurity, which is a hard reality, an actual experience. This is explained by the sage thus:

"There is nothing permanent either on earth or in ourselves. Thought can give continuity to something it thinks about. It can give permanency to a word, to an idea, to a tradition. ... It can build an image and give to that image a continuity, a permanency, calling it **ātman**, or whatever you like." (25 : 28).

In another statement the sage has said:

"To discover that nothing is permanent is of tremendous importance, for only then is the mind free, then you can look, and in that there is great joy." (21 : 75).

Another important fact about how the notion of the permanent is created by the mind is brought out by the sage thus:

"Being caught in the pain of impermanency, the mind is driven to seek the permanent, under whatever name; and its very craving for the permanent creates the permanent, which is the opposite of **what is**. So really there is no search, but only the desire to find the comforting satisfaction of the permanent." (28 : 18).

## Mahāvākya No. 12

**Thought creates the thinker.** (26 : 158).

The idea of the thinker, the 'me', the self, is a prerogative only of human beings among the whole of the animal world. It has come about with the development of the brain over millions of years in which it has come to have a much larger size proportional to the body as compared to all other beings. As a result of this, formation of new specialised areas controlling functions like storage of experience, power to revive the stored traces of experience, connecting the past with the future, forming ideas of relations in the different events taking place in the world around and, above all, having the ability to form and actually entertain such things as expectations, anxiety, fear, hypocrisy, truth and falsehood. All these abilities have contributed to the formation of a wholly new experience in the human mind, the feeling of a novel kind of entity, which is entirely imaginary, fictitious but felt as actually existing and present most intimately and unmistakably, in each experience, sensation. It is the feeling and experience of the 'I', the 'me', the 'mine', which is felt as the most tangible, most fundamental, unequivocal entity, always felt as accompanying one's own existence. The idea of one's own existence is, indeed, impossible without the 'I'. The human neonate is devoid of the 'I' or the 'me' at birth. But it starts developing quickly and is established firmly by the age of three years in one's personality as its very basis, the very foundation on which the superstructure and the whole framework of personality takes shape.

This is called the thinker. In Sanskrit, in the ancient tradition of Indian philosophy, it is called **asmitā** or **ahamkāra**. It is the vehicle of all thoughts, feelings, emotions, passions and, in fact, of all mental activities. It is felt and experienced to have a separate existence from thoughts. The thinker is taken to be there already, and thoughts may arise from time to time in it. This idea of the thinker as an entity, separately in existence, already in the thoughts arising in it, is rejected by Krishnamurti. Due to our strong habit of taking the thinker to be a basic reality underlying all thinking, we find the **mahāvākya** of Krishnamurti that 'thought creates the thinker' as strange, difficult to accept, rather unbelievable. But actually it is a very true, very significant saying. Let us see how the sage has explained it in his own words.

"Is there a perceiver or only perception? Please follow this closely. Is there a thinker or only thinking? Surely, the thinker does not exist first. First there is thinking, and then thinking creates the thinker—which means that a separation in thinking has taken place. It is when this separation takes place that there comes into being the watcher and the watched, the perceiver and the object of perception. ...When you look at a flower, when you just see it, at that moment is there an entity who sees? Or is there only seeing? Seeing the flower makes you say, 'How nice it is!' I want it. So the 'I' comes into being through desire, fear, greed, ambition, which follow in the wake of seeing. It is these that create the 'I' and the 'I' is non-existent without them." (24 : 245).

How the 'I' or the 'me' originates is explained clearly by the sage in the above passage. It comes about when I say to myself anything as a result of an experience. If nothing is said, and the experiencing takes place without naming, without any use of words, then there is no thought and, hence, no thinker. The experiencing without naming is called '**nirvikalpaka pratyaksha**' in ancient Indian philosophy. It may be called 'experiencing alone' without calling it or describing it by using words as symbols. With the use of words there is a whole chain of revival of traces of stored material in the brain cells, such as likes and dislikes, emotions, fear, desire, cravings, and so on. This is the content, the essence, of the 'me', the 'thinker'. It has no existence, no operation, no 'coming to act' without thinking, without the revival of stored material, without memory. This is explained by the sage in the following statement:

"Naming only strengthens and gives continuity to the experiencer, to the desire for permanency, to the characteristic of particularising memory. There must be silent awareness of naming and so the understanding of it. We name not only to communicate, but also to give continuity and substance to an experience, to revive it and to repeat its sensations. This naming process must cease, not only on the superficial level of the mind, but throughout its entire structure. ...Our whole consciousness is a process of naming or terming experience, and then storing or recording it. This process gives nourishment and strength to the illusory entity, the experiencer as distinct and separate from the experience. Without thought there is no thinker. Thoughts create the thinker who isolates himself to give himself permanency; for thoughts are always impermanent." (26 : 69).

This is further explained in a slightly different way in the following words:

"There is only thought, and thought creates the thinker; thought gives form to the thinker as a permanent, separate entity. ...But there is only the process of thinking, there is no thinker apart from thought. The experiencing of this truth is vital." (27 : 26).

To quote one short statement of the sage:

"The watcher and the watched are inseparable. All the qualities of the watcher are contained in his thinking. If there is no thinking, there is no watcher, no thinker. This is a fact." (28 : 53).

— — —

## Chapter 3

# Unintelligibility: A Peculiarity of the Teachings

Krishnamurti's books are usually found to leave behind in the mind of a reader a feeling of being unclear, unenlightened, on several matters, although the general tenor of his teachings seems to be well understood. The reasons for this rather strange, disappointing result may be attributed both to the speaker and writer, and to his audiences and readers. First about the readers. They usually lacked a keen intention and inclination to understand, due to their already formed habit of expecting to be told what to do positively, and how to do it. It was a pre-requisite for benefiting in any way from Krishnamurti's teachings, to be able to look into it like we look into a mirror and to observe one's own self in that mirror. Instead, they wanted to be spoon-fed, to be led step by step to the goal of enlightenment. Krishnamurti's insistence was on being a light unto oneself. Thus, there was always a wide gap between the speaker and his listeners.

On the part of the speaker, we may point out two shortcomings. One was that he was much ahead of his times. He had himself undergone a transformation, regeneration, a total inner change, a radical revolution. He always spoke from that state. He could see, look, listen, observe any situation directly, without any past, but the minds of the audiences were choked with likes and dislikes, with choice and conditioning. It seems that this situation of the mind of the common people will take one or two centuries to undergo an inner change of attitude, due to the scientific revolution that has just begun to influence the human mind. It will take some more time to remove the demand for certainty, permanence, and psychological security, so strongly ingrained at present in the human mind. When that happens, a great hurdle in understanding Krishnamurti will have been removed.

The second shortcoming on the part of the speaker was that he had never read any books on philosophy, religion, or psychology. He himself declared this very clearly at one point. (1 : 231-232). So he depended on his own vocabulary which was different from that of the common people. His talks were somewhat like a person speaking to himself. The listener was often completely at a loss to make out clearly what he was talking about. There was a linguistic barrier between the speaker and his audiences.

Here, we shall go through some of his statements which are very hard to understand. That will make these points clear.

1. "Creation is never in the hands of the individual. It ceases entirely when individuality, with its capacities, gifts, techniques and so on, becomes dominant. Creation is the movement of the unknowable essence of the whole; it is never the expression of the part." (10 : 11).

2. "Maturity is not of time and age. There is no interval between now and maturity. There is never 'in the meantime'. Maturity is that state when all choice has ceased; it is only the immature that choose and know the conflict of choice. In maturity there is no direction but there is a direction which is not a direction of choice. Conflict at any level, at any depth, indicates immaturity. There is no such thing as becoming mature, except organically, the mechanical inevitability of certain things to ripen. The understanding, which is the transcending of conflict, in all its complex varieties, is maturity." (10 : 73-74).

3. "What is the quality of the mind that can explore? I see that any partial movement is incomplete and, therefore, does not get anywhere. I see that partial seeing is no seeing at all and, therefore, I am finished with it. It is completely over. The mind then asks what the nature of perception is that is total. And it is only such a total perception that can examine. And it may not need to examine at all, because

that which has to be examined is of the partial field—division, analysis, exploration." (19 : 130-131).

4. "So it is good to be sceptical, because it gives you a chance to find out for yourself whether you need a guru at all. What is important is to be a light unto yourself, to be your own master and disciple, to be both the teacher and the pupil. As long as you are learning, there is no teacher. It is only when you have stopped exploring, discovering, understanding the whole process of life, that the teacher comes into being—and such a teacher has no value. Then you are dead and, therefore, your teacher is also dead." (29 : 48).

5. "Love is something extraordinary, is it not? You cannot love if you are thinking about yourself—which does not mean that you must think about somebody else. Love **is**, it has no object. The mind that loves is really a religious mind because it is in the movement of reality, of truth, of God, and it is only such a mind that can know what beauty is. The mind that is not caught in any philosophy, that is not enclosed in any system or belief, that is not driven by its own ambition and is, therefore, sensitive, alert, watchful—such a mind has beauty." (29 : 153).

6. "While you are young, you should awaken within yourself the flame of discontent; you should be in a state of revolution. This is the time to inquire, to discover, to grow; therefore, insist that your parents and your teachers educate you properly. Do not be satisfied merely to sit in a classroom and absorb information about this king or that war. Be discontented, go to your teachers and inquire, find out. If they are not intelligent, by inquiring, you will help them to be intelligent; and when you leave the school, you will be growing into maturity, into real freedom. Then you will continue to learn right through life till you die, and you will be a happy, intelligent human being." (12 : 34-35).

7. "What is important is for you to go behind the word 'love' to see whether you actually do love your parents, and whether your parents do actually love you. Surely, if you and your

parents really loved one another, the world would be entirely different. There would be no wars, no starvation, no class differences. There would be no rich and no poor. You see, without love we try to reform society economically, we try to put things right; but as long as we have no love in our hearts, we cannot bring about a social structure free of conflict and misery. That is why we have to go into these things very carefully, and perhaps then we shall find out what love is." (12 : 73).

8. "In consciousness, there is the good and the bad; the bad is increasing; it is increasing because the good has become static, the good is not flowering. One has accepted certain patterns of what is thought to be good and one lives according to these patterns. So, the good, instead of flowering, is withering and thereby giving strength to the bad. There is more violence, more hatred, there are more national and religious divisions, there is every form of antagonism, right through the world. It is on the increase because the good is not flowering. Now, be aware of this fact without any effort; the moment one makes effort, one gives importance to the self, which is the bad. Just observe the actual fact of the bad without any effort. Observe it without any choice—because choice is a distorting factor. When one observes so openly, so freely, then the good begins to flower. It is not that one pursues the good and thereby gives it strength to flower but when the bad, the evil, the ugly, is understood, completely, the other naturally flowers." (17 : 157-158).

9. "Love is not time; it is not a remembrance. If it is, it is not love, obviously. 'I love you because you gave me sex, or you gave me food, or flattered me; or you said you needed a companion; I am lonely, therefore, I need you,'—all that is not love, surely? ...Love is obviously a state of mind in which there is no verbalisation, no remembrance, but something immediate. There is a way of living in daily life where time as movement from this state to that has gone. What happens when you do that? You have an extraordinary vitality, an extraordinary sense of clarity. You are then only

dealing with facts, not with ideas. But as most of us are imprisoned in ideas, and have accepted that way of life, it is very difficult to break away. But have an insight into it, then it is finished." (17 : 174-175).

10. "Life is destruction, life is love, life is creation. We know none of it. It is a tremendous thing. ...It is a very delicate thing, a subtle thing, to have capacity and not to be slave to it, to respond immediately to things you have to respond to, and to have this extraordinary depth and height and width. Deny the little. Do you know what it is to deny? Deny not because you have got the long vision but because what is denied is false." (9 : 64-65).

11. "You, sir, are the rest of humanity, psychologically, deeply. Your reactions are shared by all humanity. Your brain is not yours, it has evolved through centuries of time. ....We are questioning deeply, whether there is an individual at all. We are the whole of humanity. We are the rest of mankind. This is not a romantic, fantastic statement, and it is important, necessary when we are going to talk over together the meaning of death. ...Time is the enemy of perception." (11 : 30).

12. "The 'me' can never become a better 'me'. It will attempt to, it thinks it can, but the 'me' remains in subtle forms. The self hides in many garments, in many structures: it varies from time to time, but there is always this self, this separative, self-centred activity which imagines that one day it will make itself something which it is not. So one sees there is no becoming of the self, there is only the ending of selfishness, of anxiety, of pain and sorrow which are the content of the psyche, of the 'me'. There is only the ending of all that, and that ending does not require time. It isn't that it will all end the day after tomorrow. It will only end when there is the perception of its movement. To perceive not only objectively, without any prejudice, bias, but to perceive without all the accumulations of the past; to witness all this without the watcher. ...Remembrances, however pleasurable, have no reality, they are things of the past, gone, finished, dead: only in observing without the

observer, who is the past, does one see the nature of time and the ending of time." (11 : 41).

These passages provide examples of verbally clear but hard to follow, difficult to grasp, perceptions of the sage. Every reader may find many such examples while reading any book of J. Krishnamurti. Some of his expressions do need clarifications. We feel that there are some missing links. If they are provided, then our understanding of what Krishnamurti tried to convey to us may be improved. The main aim of this book is to provide those missing links. Of course, that can help only those who have a keen interest and intention to understand.

In the next chapter, we shall discuss 187 problems of human life selected from Krishnamurti's writings.

— — —

## Chapter 4

# Problems of Human Life

The 187 problems chosen for description in this book have been discussed several times by J. Krishnamurti in his talks and writings. Among them some problems are intimately related with each other like, for example, transformation, regeneration, revolution, and mutation, or problems like fragmentation, division, isolation and corner of the field. Some of them are just synonymous, e.g., discovery, perception, enlightenment, experiencing, seeing the false as the false. If we consider such problems together in a group, along with each other, then our understanding of all of them improves and becomes easy. The 187 problems are, therefore, divided under 27 different groups on the basis of affinity with each other. There is a varying number of problems under each group. They are all arranged alphabetically in each group. We have formed two lists of the problems. In the first list, all the 187 problems are arranged alphabetically, giving the group number and position in that group of each one of them. The second list contains groups from number 1 to number 27. In each group, the problems are mentioned alphabetically, also giving the position of that problem in the first list, in a round bracket.

### LIST NO. 1

### 187 Problems of Human Life

| *Sl. No.* | *Name* | *Group* | *Position* |
|---|---|---|---|
| 1. | Aloneness | 1 | 1 |
| 2. | Ambition | 18 | 1 |
| 3. | Anger | 18 | 2 |
| 4. | Anonymity | 13 | 1 |

| Sl. No. | Name | Group | Position |
|---|---|---|---|
| 5. | Atman | 21 | 1 |
| 6. | Attachment | 2 | 1 |
| 7. | Attention | 14 | 1 |
| 8. | Austerity | 13 | 2 |
| 9. | Authority | 15 | 1 |
| 10. | Awareness | 14 | 2 |
| 11. | Becoming | 5 | 1 |
| 12. | Belief | 16 | 1 |
| 13. | Benediction | 6 | 1 |
| 14. | Bliss | 6 | 2 |
| 15. | Body | 12 | 1 |
| 16. | Bondage | 16 | 2 |
| 17. | Brain | 23 | 1 |
| 18. | Brain cells | 23 | 2 |
| 19. | Celibacy | 5 | 2 |
| 20. | Centre | 11 | 1 |
| 21. | Certainty | 21 | 2 |
| 22. | Chattering mind | 18 | 3 |
| 23. | Comparison | 18 | 4 |
| 24. | Concentration | 18 | 5 |
| 25. | Conclusion | 16 | 3 |
| 26. | Conditioning | 16 | 4 |
| 27. | Conflict | 18 | 6 |
| 28. | Conformity | 15 | 2 |
| 29. | Consciousness | 23 | 3 |
| 30. | Content of consciousness | 23 | 4 |
| 31. | Contradiction | 18 | 7 |
| 32. | Corner of the field | 19 | 1 |
| 33. | Craving | 2 | 2 |
| 34. | Creativeness | 13 | 3 |

| *Sl. No.* | *Name* | *Group* | *Position* |
|---|---|---|---|
| 35. | Death | 1 | 2 |
| 36. | Denial | 1 | 3 |
| 37. | Desire | 2 | 3 |
| 38. | Direct experience | 14 | 3 |
| 39. | Direct perception | 10 | 1 |
| 40. | Discipline | 5 | 3 |
| 41. | Discovery | 10 | 2 |
| 42. | Disorder | 18 | 8 |
| 43. | Distraction | 18 | 9 |
| 44. | Division | 19 | 2 |
| 45. | Dogma | 16 | 5 |
| 46. | Doubt | 17 | 1 |
| 47. | Dreams | 16 | 6 |
| 48. | Dying to the past | 1 | 4 |
| 49. | Education | 17 | 2 |
| 50. | Effort | 5 | 4 |
| 51. | Emptiness | 1 | 5 |
| 52. | Ending of self | 11 | 2 |
| 53. | Ending of sorrow | 25 | 1 |
| 54. | Ending of thought | 25 | 2 |
| 55. | Ending of time | 25 | 3 |
| 56. | Energy | 26 | 1 |
| 57. | Enlightenment | 10 | 3 |
| 58. | Escapes | 18 | 10 |
| 59. | Experience | 23 | 5 |
| 60. | Experiencer | 11 | 3 |
| 61. | Experiencing | 10 | 4 |
| 62. | False as the false | 10 | 5 |
| 63. | Fear | 2 | 4 |
| 64. | First step is the last step | 1 | 6 |

| *Sl. No.* | *Name* | *Group* | *Position* |
|---|---|---|---|
| 65. | Following another | 15 | 3 |
| 66. | Fragmentation | 19 | 3 |
| 67. | Freedom | 1 | 7 |
| 68. | Fresh mind | 6 | 3 |
| 69. | Goals | 7 | 1 |
| 70. | God | 21 | 3 |
| 71. | Gratification | 4 | 1 |
| 72. | Greed | 2 | 5 |
| 73. | Guru | 20 | 1 |
| 74. | Habit | 16 | 7 |
| 75. | Happiness | 4 | 2 |
| 76. | Holy | 3 | 1 |
| 77. | Human life | 27 | 1 |
| 78. | Human mind | 27 | 2 |
| 79. | Humility | 13 | 4 |
| 80. | How | 27 | 3 |
| 81. | Idea | 7 | 2 |
| 82. | Ideals | 7 | 3 |
| 83. | Identification | 2 | 6 |
| 84. | Ignorance | 16 | 8 |
| 85. | Illusion | 16 | 9 |
| 86. | Image | 7 | 4 |
| 87. | Impermanence | 21 | 4 |
| 88. | Innocence | 13 | 5 |
| 89. | Insight | 10 | 6 |
| 90. | Isolation | 19 | 4 |
| 91. | Integrally intelligent | 17 | 3 |
| 92. | Intelligence | 22 | 1 |
| 93. | Intention to find out | 27 | 4 |
| 94. | Intention to understand | 27 | 5 |

| *Sl. No.* | *Name* | *Group* | *Position* |
|---|---|---|---|
| 95. | Joy | 6 | 4 |
| 96. | Knowing oneself | 14 | 4 |
| 97. | Knowledge | 23 | 6 |
| 98. | Known | 23 | 7 |
| 99. | Learning | 17 | 4 |
| 100. | Light unto oneself | 15 | 4 |
| 101. | Listening | 17 | 5 |
| 102. | Loneliness | 1 | 8 |
| 103. | Looking | 17 | 6 |
| 104. | Love | 22 | 2 |
| 105. | Master | 20 | 2 |
| 106. | Me | 11 | 4 |
| 107. | Meditation | 8 | 1 |
| 108. | Memory | 23 | 8 |
| 109. | Mind | 23 | 9 |
| 110. | Mind made still | 5 | 5 |
| 111. | Monk | 20 | 3 |
| 112. | Mutation | 24 | 1 |
| 113. | Naming | 7 | 5 |
| 114. | Negation | 1 | 9 |
| 115. | New | 6 | 5 |
| 116. | Nothingness | 13 | 6 |
| 117. | Now | 13 | 7 |
| 118. | Observation | 10 | 7 |
| 119. | Observed | 9 | 1 |
| 120. | Observer | 11 | 5 |
| 121. | Occupied mind | 18 | 11 |
| 122. | Opinion | 16 | 10 |
| 123. | Opposites | 18 | 12 |
| 124. | Order | 22 | 3 |

| *Sl. No.* | *Name* | *Group* | *Position* |
|---|---|---|---|
| 125. | Others can't help | 15 | 5 |
| 126. | Outsider | 1 | 10 |
| 127. | Passion | 26 | 2 |
| 128. | Passive awareness | 13 | 8 |
| 129. | Past | 23 | 10 |
| 130. | Pathless truth | 15 | 6 |
| 131. | Perception | 10 | 8 |
| 132. | Permanence | 21 | 5 |
| 133. | Pleasure | 4 | 3 |
| 134. | Practice | 5 | 6 |
| 135. | Prayer | 5 | 7 |
| 136. | Prison | 16 | 11 |
| 137. | Quiet mind | 8 | 2 |
| 138. | Reality | 9 | 2 |
| 139. | Regeneration | 24 | 2 |
| 140. | Relationship | 27 | 6 |
| 141. | Religion | 5 | 8 |
| 142. | Renunciation | 5 | 9 |
| 143. | Revolution | 24 | 3 |
| 144. | Ritual | 5 | 10 |
| 145. | Sacred | 3 | 2 |
| 146. | Saint | 20 | 4 |
| 147. | Sannyasi | 20 | 5 |
| 148. | Saviour | 20 | 6 |
| 149. | Second-hand | 27 | 7 |
| 150. | Security | 21 | 6 |
| 151. | Seeing | 17 | 7 |
| 152. | Seeking | 18 | 13 |
| 153. | Self | 11 | 6 |
| 154. | Self-abandonment | 13 | 9 |

| *Sl. No.* | *Name* | *Group* | *Position* |
|---|---|---|---|
| 155. | Self-deception | 16 | 12 |
| 156. | Self-knowledge | 14 | 5 |
| 157. | Self-pity | 27 | 8 |
| 158. | Sensitiveness | 13 | 10 |
| 159. | Silence | 8 | 3 |
| 160. | Simplicity | 13 | 11 |
| 161. | Solitude | 1 | 11 |
| 162. | Sorrow | 27 | 9 |
| 163. | Space | 8 | 4 |
| 164. | Spontaneity | 14 | 6 |
| 165. | Stillness | 8 | 5 |
| 166. | Symbols | 7 | 6 |
| 167. | Thinker | 11 | 7 |
| 168. | Thought | 23 | 11 |
| 169. | Time | 27 | 10 |
| 170. | Total action | 17 | 8 |
| 171. | Total attention | 17 | 9 |
| 172. | Tradition | 23 | 12 |
| 173. | Tranquillity | 8 | 6 |
| 174. | Transformation | 24 | 4 |
| 175. | Truth | 9 | 3 |
| 176. | Uncertainty | 21 | 7 |
| 177. | Understanding | 22 | 4 |
| 178. | Unknown | 9 | 4 |
| 179. | Violence | 27 | 11 |
| 180. | Virtue | 5 | 11 |
| 181. | Vision | 16 | 13 |
| 182. | What is | 9 | 5 |
| 183. | What should be | 18 | 14 |
| 184. | Wisdom | 22 | 5 |

| Sl. No. | Name | Group | Position |
|---|---|---|---|
| 185. | Words | 7 | 7 |
| 186. | Worship | 5 | 12 |
| 187. | You are the world | 27 | 12 |

## LIST NO. 2

### Group No. 1

| | | |
|---|---|---|
| 1-1 | (1) | Aloneness |
| 1-2 | (35) | Death |
| 1-3 | (36) | Denial |
| 1-4 | (48) | Dying to the past |
| 1-5 | (51) | Emptiness |
| 1-6 | (64) | First step is the last step |
| 1-7 | (67) | Freedom |
| 1-8 | (102) | Loneliness |
| 1-9 | (114) | Negation |
| 1-10 | (126) | Outsider |
| 1-11 | (161) | Solitude |

### Group No. 2

| | | |
|---|---|---|
| 2-1 | (6) | Attachment |
| 2-2 | (33) | Craving |
| 2-3 | (37) | Desire |
| 2-4 | (63) | Fear |
| 2-5 | (72) | Greed |
| 2-6 | (83) | Identification |

### Group No. 3

| | | |
|---|---|---|
| 3-1 | (76) | Holy |
| 3-2 | (145) | Sacred |

## Group No. 4

| | | |
|---|---|---|
| 4-1 | (71) | Gratification |
| 4-2 | (75) | Happiness |
| 4-3 | (133) | Pleasure |

## Group No. 5

| | | |
|---|---|---|
| 5-1 | (11) | Becoming |
| 5-2 | (19) | Celibacy |
| 5-3 | (40) | Discipline |
| 5-4 | (50) | Effort |
| 5-5 | (110) | Mind made still |
| 5-6 | (134) | Practice |
| 5-7 | (135) | Prayer |
| 5-8 | (141) | Religion |
| 5-9 | (142) | Renunciation |
| 5-10 | (144) | Ritual |
| 5-11 | (180) | Virtue |
| 5-12 | (186) | Worship |

## Group No. 6

| | | |
|---|---|---|
| 6-1 | (13) | Benediction |
| 6-2 | (14) | Bliss |
| 6-3 | (68) | Fresh mind |
| 6-4 | (95) | Joy |
| 6-5 | (115) | New |

## Group No. 7

| | | |
|---|---|---|
| 7-1 | (69) | Goals |
| 7-2 | (81) | Idea |
| 7-3 | (82) | Ideals |
| 7-4 | (86) | Image |
| 7-5 | (113) | Naming |

| | | |
|---|---|---|
| 7-6 | (166) | Symbols |
| 7-7 | (185) | Words |

## Group No. 8

| | | |
|---|---|---|
| 8-1 | (107) | Meditation |
| 8-2 | (137) | Quiet mind |
| 8-3 | (159) | Silence |
| 8-4 | (163) | Space |
| 8-5 | (165) | Stillness |
| 8-6 | (173) | Tranquillity |

## Group No. 9

| | | |
|---|---|---|
| 9-1 | (119) | Observed |
| 9-2 | (138) | Reality |
| 9-3 | (175) | Truth |
| 9-4 | (178) | Unknown |
| 9-5 | (182) | What is |

## Group No. 10

| | | |
|---|---|---|
| 10-1 | (39) | Direct perception |
| 10-2 | (41) | Discovery |
| 10-3 | (57) | Enlightenment |
| 10-4 | (61) | Experiencing |
| 10-5 | (62) | False as the false |
| 10-6 | (89) | Insight |
| 10-7 | (118) | Observation |
| 10-8 | (131) | Perception |

## Group No. 11

| | | |
|---|---|---|
| 11-1 | (20) | Centre |
| 11-2 | (52) | Ending of self |
| 11-3 | (60) | Experiencer |

| | | |
|---|---|---|
| 11-4 | (106) | Me |
| 11-5 | (120) | Observer |
| 11-6 | (153) | Self |
| 11-7 | (167) | Thinker |

## Group No. 12

| | | |
|---|---|---|
| 12-1 | (15) | Body |

## Group No. 13

| | | |
|---|---|---|
| 13-1 | (4) | Anonymity |
| 13-2 | (8) | Austerity |
| 13-3 | (34) | Creativeness |
| 13-4 | (79) | Humility |
| 13-5 | (88) | Innocence |
| 13-6 | (116) | Nothingness |
| 13-7 | (117) | Now |
| 13-8 | (128) | Passive awareness |
| 13-9 | (154) | Self-abandonment |
| 13-10 | (158) | Sensitiveness |
| 13-11 | (160) | Simplicity |

## Group No. 14

| | | |
|---|---|---|
| 14-1 | (7) | Attention |
| 14-2 | (10) | Awareness |
| 14-3 | (38) | Direct experience |
| 14-4 | (96) | Knowing oneself |
| 14-5 | (156) | Self-knowledge |
| 14-6 | (164) | Spontaneity |

## Group No. 15

| | | |
|---|---|---|
| 15-1 | (9) | Authority |
| 15-2 | (28) | Conformity |

| | | |
|---|---|---|
| 15-3 | (65) | Following another |
| 15-4 | (100) | Light unto oneself |
| 15-5 | (125) | Others can't help |
| 15-6 | (130) | Pathless truth |

## Group No. 16

| | | |
|---|---|---|
| 16-1 | (12) | Belief |
| 16-2 | (16) | Bondage |
| 16-3 | (25) | Conclusion |
| 16-4 | (26) | Conditioning |
| 16-5 | (45) | Dogma |
| 16-6 | (47) | Dreams |
| 16-7 | (74) | Habit |
| 16-8 | (84) | Ignorance |
| 16-9 | (85) | Illusions |
| 16-10 | (122) | Opinion |
| 16-11 | (136) | Prison |
| 16-12 | (155) | Self-deception |
| 16-13 | (181) | Visions |

## Group No. 17

| | | |
|---|---|---|
| 17-1 | (46) | Doubt |
| 17-2 | (49) | Education |
| 17-3 | (91) | Integrally intelligent |
| 17-4 | (99) | Learning |
| 17-5 | (101) | Listening |
| 17-6 | (103) | Looking |
| 17-7 | (151) | Seeing |
| 17-8 | (170) | Total action |
| 17-9 | (171) | Total attention |

## Group No. 18

| | | |
|---|---|---|
| 18-1 | (2) | Ambition |
| 18-2 | (3) | Anger |
| 18-3 | (22) | Chattering mind |
| 18-4 | (23) | Comparison |
| 18-5 | (24) | Concentration |
| 18-6 | (27) | Conflict |
| 18-7 | (31) | Contradiction |
| 18-8 | (42) | Disorder |
| 18-9 | (43) | Distraction |
| 18-10 | (58) | Escapes |
| 18-11 | (121) | Occupied mind |
| 18-12 | (123) | Opposites |
| 18-13 | (152) | Seeking |
| 18-14 | (183) | What should be |

## Group No. 19

| | | |
|---|---|---|
| 19-1 | (32) | Corner of the field |
| 19-2 | (44) | Division |
| 19-3 | (66) | Fragmentation |
| 19-4 | (90) | Isolation |

## Group No. 20

| | | |
|---|---|---|
| 20-1 | (73) | Guru |
| 20-2 | (105) | Master |
| 20-3 | (111) | Monk |
| 20-4 | (146) | Saint |
| 20-5 | (147) | Sannyasi |
| 20-6 | (148) | Saviour |

## Group No. 21

| | | |
|---|---|---|
| 21-1 | (5) | Atman |

| | | |
|---|---|---|
| 21-2 | (21) | Certainty |
| 21-3 | (70) | God |
| 21-4 | (87) | Impermanence |
| 21-5 | (132) | Permanence |
| 21-6 | (150) | Security |
| 21-7 | (176) | Uncertainty |

## Group No. 22

| | | |
|---|---|---|
| 22-1 | (92) | Intelligence |
| 22-2 | (104) | Love |
| 22-3 | (124) | Order |
| 22-4 | (177) | Understanding |
| 22-5 | (184) | Wisdom |

## Group No. 23

| | | |
|---|---|---|
| 23-1 | (17) | Brain |
| 23-2 | (18) | Brain cells |
| 23-3 | (29) | Consciousness |
| 23-4 | (30) | Content of consciousness |
| 23-5 | (59) | Experience |
| 23-6 | (97) | Knowledge |
| 23-7 | (98) | Known |
| 23-8 | (108) | Memory |
| 23-9 | (109) | Mind |
| 23-10 | (129) | Past |
| 23-11 | (168) | Thought |
| 23-12 | (172) | Tradition |

## Group No. 24

| | | |
|---|---|---|
| 24-1 | (112) | Mutation |
| 24-2 | (139) | Regeneration |
| 24-3 | (143) | Revolution |
| 24-4 | (174) | Transformation |

## Group No. 25

| | | |
|---|---|---|
| 25-1 | (53) | Ending of sorrow |
| 25-2 | (54) | Ending of thought |
| 25-3 | (55) | Ending of time |

## Group No. 26

| | | |
|---|---|---|
| 26-1 | (56) | Energy |
| 26-2 | (127) | Passion |

## Group No. 27

| | | |
|---|---|---|
| 27-1 | (77) | Human life |
| 27-2 | (78) | Human mind |
| 27-3 | (80) | How |
| 27-4 | (93) | Intention to find out |
| 27-5 | (94) | Intention to understand |
| 27-6 | (140) | Relationship |
| 27-7 | (149) | Second hand |
| 27-8 | (157) | Self-pity |
| 27-9 | (162) | Sorrow |
| 27-10 | (169) | Time |
| 27-11 | (179) | Violence |
| 27-12 | (187) | You are the world |

# 187 PROBLEMS OF HUMAN LIFE

## 1-1 (1) ALONENESS

**See under Mahāvākya No. 8, Chapter 2.**

## 1-2 (35) DEATH

Death is a hard reality of life of every living being. Every one of us is afraid of death. It puts an end to all that we know, we have, we desire, and we fear. The desire that our body, our life, should not come to an end, which is called 'clinging to life', is called '**abhinivesha**' in the Yogasūtra of Patanjali. It is one of the five basic, ingrained tendencies of the human mind, known as the five **kleshas**. They are: (*i*) ignorance (**avidyā**), (*ii*) ego-feeling (**asmitā**), (*iii*) attachment (**rāga**), (*iv*) aversion (**dvesha**), and (*v*) fear of death or clinging to life (**abhinivesha**). (Yogasūtra-II : 3). The famous Sanskrit poet Kalidasa has described death as a basic nature of living beings (**maranam prakritih sharirinām**) (Raghuvamsha VIII : 87). We are reminded of the possibility and inevitability of our own death many a time in our life, but we tend to forget it quickly and get attached again to our life activities.

Krishnamurti used the word, death, in two different senses, one like the commonly attributed meaning, as mentioned above. The other meaning was indicated by the phrases 'dying to the past' or 'dying to the known'. Here death meant putting the past experiences aside, being free from them. This has been a very crucial concept of Krishnamurti's teachings, which we come across again and again. It means the same thing as 'freedom from the known'. That meaning will be clear from the **Problem 1-4 (48): Dying to the past**.

"There is this preoccupation with death because we are afraid to lose the known, the things that we have gathered... If we could carry over all the things that we have gathered—our friends, our possessions, our virtues, our character—then we would not be afraid of death, would we? That is why we invent theories about death and the hereafter. But the fear is that death is the ending, and most of us are unwilling to face this fact. We don't want to leave the known; so it is our clinging to the known that creates fear in us, not the unknown." (24 : 243).

In the above statement, the word 'death' has been used with the usual, common meaning.

Krishnamurti has differentiated between the death of the body and death of the mind. For example, he has said:

"Sooner or later there is the death of the body, but most of us have minds which are already dead." (24 : 139).

By death of the mind, he means the lack of sensitivity, the tendency to imitate others, to conform, to follow a pattern. It is very important to understand these states, which Krishnamurti takes to be indicative of the death of one's mind.

## 1-3 (36) DENIAL

Denial means the refusal to adopt or accept something. Krishnamurti has used this word in the sense of being free from what is false, conditioned, illusory. It is synonymous in his teachings with aloneness, freedom, emptiness and negation. The following statements would make this clear:

"To deny is to be alone; alone from all influence, tradition, and from need. ...To be alone is to deny the conditioning, the background. ...Aloneness is not withdrawal from life; on the contrary, it is the total freedom from conflict and sorrow, from fear and death. ...This aloneness is emptiness. ...In this fire of emptiness the mind is made young, fresh and innocent." (10 : 111).

"To deny and to remain with the denial in negation is action without motive, which is love." (10 : 217).

## 1-4 (48) DYING TO THE PAST

This is a very peculiar phrase put together by J. Krishnamurti. Here he uses the word 'death' in the sense of completely abandoning past accumulations, ideas, notions, experiences, due to understanding '**what is**' completely. He has said:

"The mind must die to everything it has gathered—to all the habits, the imitated virtues, to all the things it has relied upon for its sense of security. Then it is no longer caught in the net of its own thinking. In dying to the past from moment to moment the mind is made fresh, therefore it can never deteriorate or set in motion the wave of darkness." (24 : 141).

At another place, he has described dying of the known as the essence of meditation.

"Death is the flowering of the new; meditation is the dying of the known." (10 : 207).

In the following statement, he explains death in the unusual sense, meaning dying to the past or the known:

"Find out what it means to die, not physically, but to everything that is known—to your family, to your attachment, to all the things that you have accumulated: the known pleasures, the known fears; **die**—so that the mind is made fresh, young, and, therefore, innocent." (13 : 13).

## 1-5 (51) EMPTINESS

Krishnamurti has used this word to mean two things which are very different from each other:

(*i*) as a feeling of vacuum, void, insufficiency, inadequacy, lack of what is desired, loneliness, uneasiness. See under **1-8 (102) LONELINESS**.

(*ii*) the other meaning is Krishnamurti's favourite meaning. See under **8-4 (163) SPACE**.

## 1-6 (64) FIRST STEP IS THE LAST STEP

This is a very crucial fact which only Krishnamurti, among all the sages, has emphasised. For understanding this, one must be able to put aside one's habit of thinking according to which one is brought up to believe very firmly that one has to go through a process of spiritual progress step by step under the guidance of a guru, i.e., through many steps, through many births, in order to reach the goal of emancipation. This, according to Krishnamurti, is a grossly mistaken notion. There is, as he says, no ultimate, absolute truth, no way or path, no steps, no method. There is only one step, the only step, and it is, indeed, the last step. This is explained by the sage thus:

"Die to the thing that is true. Otherwise it becomes memory, which then becomes thought. ...If the mind sees clearly and it can only see clearly when the seeing is the ending of it, then the mind can start a movement where the first step is the last step." (19 : 29).

"All systems offer a process, a fixed point and the ending of all trouble. ...Can the mind, seeing something very clearly, end that perception? Then here the very first step is the last step. The mind is fresh to look." (19 : 31).

This point will become clear further in the next problem, that of freedom.

## 1-7 (67) FREEDOM

**See under Mahāvākya No. 9, Chapter 2.**

## 1-8 (102) LONELINESS

Loneliness or inner emptiness involves a kind of uneasiness which stands out as one of the most fundamental, difficult and widespread problems of human life. It is a state of human mind that is very different from aloneness or solitude, which always occurred prominently in Krishnamurti's discourses. This problem appears almost impossible to solve for most of us. It can be resolved, as explained by the sage, only by understanding desire and by self-knowledge.

"What a strange thing is loneliness and how frightening it is ...We will do anything to escape from loneliness, to cover it up. ...You may lose yourself in a crowd and yet be utterly lonely. ...Put the book down, and it is there. Amusements and drinks cannot drown loneliness; you may temporarily evade it, but when the laughter and the effects of alcohol are over, the fear of loneliness returns. ...The craving to fill this emptiness—or to run away from it, which is the same thing—cannot be sublimated or suppressed." (26 : 103-104).

"I am afraid of my loneliness. I never examine my loneliness—what it means—but I am afraid of it, which means I run away from it, but that loneliness is my shadow, it pursues me. ...You have to understand time. If you understand time, then perhaps there will be an end to fear." (15 : 11).

## 1-9 (114) NEGATION

Negation is a word quite similar in meaning to other words like aloneness, denial, emptiness, freedom, solitude and outsider, included by us in group no. 1. To negate means not to accept, to do away with, to deny, to be empty, i.e., having space, to be free, to remain away from or outside of. What is it that one is to be outside of, or free from? Indeed, it is the accumulation of past experiences, knowledge gained from others, opinions and conclusions formed from it. This freedom, negation, denial is the very first step. It is the only step. It is the last step, because there is no further step, no effort or discipline called for. It makes the mind quiet and such a quiet mind alone can look, see, observe directly, without any mediation of the past, that is to say, immediately. It can come upon **what is**. This is, in short, what the sage has said repeatedly. Let us see this truth in his own words:

"It is only when there is emptiness in oneself, not the emptiness of a shallow mind, but the emptiness that comes with total negation of everything one has been and should be and will be—it is only in this emptiness that there is creation. It is only in this emptiness that something new can take place. ...Can you negate yourself completely? If not, there is no freedom." (25 : 282-283).

"Through negation you come upon the positive, but if you pursue the positive, it leads you to a dead end." (13 : 14-15).

This statement of the sage regarding negation must be understood very clearly. Positive means the efforts, discipline, **sādhanā** of yoga, and taught by the yogis. The sage has said:

"Please follow this clearly. In the very understanding of what is disorder, there comes freedom which brings about order. ...That is, to understand negatively is to bring about a positive act. Not through pursuing a positive pattern will order come. There is disorder. This disorder is caused by man pursuing a certain pattern—a social pattern, an ethical pattern, a religious pattern, a pattern which is based on his own personal inclination or pleasure, and so on. ...Order is imposed upon us—which brings disorder. In the understanding of that there is a discipline which brings about order." (20 : 64).

## 1-10 (126) OUTSIDER

A very clear description of what 'being an outsider' means is found in the following statement of the sage:

"There is a difference between isolation, cutting oneself off, and aloneness, solitude. ...To be alone you must die to the past. When you are alone, totally alone ...there is that sense of being an outsider. The man who is completely alone in this way is innocent and it is this innocence that frees the mind from sorrow.

...Only such a mind can see that which is truth and that which is not measurable by words. In this solitude, you will begin to understand the necessity of living with yourself as you are, not as you think you should be or as you have been." (21 : 69).

## 1-11 (161) SOLITUDE

Solitude means being alone. It is explained by the sage in the following two statements:

"For the total development of the human being, solitude as a means of cultivating sensitivity becomes a necessity. One has to know what it is to be alone, what it is to meditate, what it is to die, and the implications of solitude, of meditation, of death can be known only by seeking them out." (12 : 14).

"That is what we do. We carry our burdens all the time; we never die to them, we never leave them behind. It is only when we give complete attention to a problem and solve it immediately—never carrying it over to the next day, the next minute—that there is solitude. Then, even if we live in a crowded house, or are in a bus, we have solitude. And that solitude indicates a fresh mind, an innocent mind." (21 : 106).

# GROUP NO. 2

## 2-1 (6) ATTACHMENT

Attachment means liking for, dependence on, mental involvement with something. It is a natural tendency of the human mind. We are attached to several things, such as property, money, power, importance in society, beliefs, goals, and so on. Our country, religion, tradition may, in many cases, be an object of attachment. Krishnamurti has brought out the fact that our conditioning, the prison that we build around ourselves, is really constituted by attachment.

"Conditioning is attachment; attachment to work, to tradition, to property, to people, to ideas and so on. If there were no attachment, would there be conditioning? Of course not. So why are we attached? I am attached to my country because through identification with it I become somebody. ...The object of attachment offers me the means of escape from my own emptiness. Attachment is escape, and it is escape that strengthens conditioning. ...It is these escapes and our attachment to them that make for conditioning. Conditioning brings problems, conflict. ...One can be free from conditioning only by understanding, being aware of our escapes." (27 : 5-6).

At another place he has said:

"Do you understand what is freedom? That is, if I am attached to a belief, to a person, to a house, I am not free. ...Why are human beings right through the world attached: to God, to a belief, to a house, to their wives, ...why?" (8 : 4).

## 2-2 (33) CRAVING

Craving means a strong, compelling desire. It usually remains unfulfilled, and so it continues prompting us to behave in various ways. It is called '**trishnā**' or '**vāsanā**' in Sanskrit. It is looked upon as the main cause of misery in human life. Krishnamurti has brought out an important fact about craving, namely, that craving and one who craves are not two separate entities. They are one. The other important point explained by him is that unless craving is understood, illusion is bound to continue. Here are his own words about these two points:

"The objects of craving may vary. You may change the object of your craving from drink to ideation; but without understanding the process of craving, illusion is inevitable. There is no entity separate from craving; there is only craving. There is no one who craves." (26 : 104-105).

**For more information, see under 2-3 (37) DESIRE.**

## 2-3 (37) DESIRE

If human life would have been such that all our desires could be satisfied as they arose, and no desire was left unfulfilled, then happiness, an unbroken chain of happy moments, could be an unmistakable, universal mark of human life. But reality is very different from this utopian idea. In our life most of our desires, a large proportion of them, remains unfulfilled or only partly fulfilled. That is the cause of a great deal of misery and suffering. Krishnamurti has pointed out some important facts about desire. It would be very beneficial to understand them thoroughly.

"Belief and knowledge are very intimately related to desire, and perhaps if we can understand these two issues, we can see how desire works and understand its complexities." (24 : 34).

"Can the mind be free from the desire for security? That is the problem." (24 : 37).

"It is only through understanding the whole process of desire that the mind can be free." (12 : 9).

"Most of us think that possessing very little indicates freedom from desire. ...But that again is a very superficial reaction. ...Your mind is crippled with innumerable wants, innumerable desires, beliefs, struggles. Surely, it is **there** that the revolution must take place, not in how much you possess or what clothes you wear or how many meals you eat." (24 : 74).

"Beyond the physical needs, **any** form of desire—for greatness, for truth, for virtue—becomes a psychological process by which the mind builds the idea of the 'me' and strengthens itself at the centre." (24 : 76).

"It is this desire for more, this dissatisfaction, which makes one accept or have faith in something, and this must inevitably lead to every form of deception and illusion. It is desire and fear, hope and despair, that project the goal, the conclusion to be experienced. Therefore this experience has no reality. All so-called religious experiences follow this pattern. The very desire for enlightenment must also breed the acceptance of authority, and this is the opposite of enlightenment. Desire, dissatisfaction, fear, pleasure, wanting more, wanting to change, all of which is measurement—this is the way of illusion." (25 : 281).

This last passage appears to be a masterpiece in which many important, significant, very valuable aspects of the teachings of J. Krishnamurti have come together. Any inquisitive person, who wants to understand Krishnamurti adequately and clearly, would do well to remember this passage always.

## 2-4 (63) FEAR

Desire and fear are both very intricate and troublesome problems of human life. They are related very intimately with each other. They are always found together. If desire is understood, negated, overcome, then fear also vanishes. Both exist with reference to some object, never without it. In Krishnamurti's discourses, fear, like desire, had an important place. It is essential to understand properly the basic facts about fear brought about by him in the following statements:

"Fear is not to be put away by appeasements and candles; it ends with the cessation of the desire to become." (26 : 67).

"You cannot replace fear with something else; if you do, fear is still there. You may successfully cover it up or run away from it, but fear remains. It is the elimination of fear, and not the finding of a substitute for it, that is important. Discipline in any form whatsoever can never bring freedom from fear. Fear has to be observed, studied, understood. Fear is not an abstraction; it comes into being only in relation to something, and it is this relationship that has to be understood. To understand is not to resist or oppose." (27 : 48-49).

This is another masterpiece of the sage to be understood watchfully. The intimate relation between fear and the 'me' is explained below:

"Thought has created a centre as the 'me'—me, my opinion, my country, my God, my experience, my house ...you know, 'me', 'me', 'me'. That is the centre from which you act. ...Can the mind look at fear without the centre? Can you look at that fear without naming it? ...It requires tremendous discipline. Then the mind is looking without the centre to which it has been accustomed and there is the ending of fear, both the hidden and the open." (6 : 68-69).

"Until we are free from fear, climb the highest mountain, invent every kind of God, we will always remain in darkness. ...One of the major causes of fear is that we do not want to face ourselves as we are." (21 : 40-41).

## 2-5 (72) GREED

Greed is one of the six great enemies (**shadripu**) of man. They are: (*i*) uncontrolled sexual desire (**kāma**), (*ii*) anger (**krodha**), (*iii*) greed (**lobha**), (*iv*) infatuation (**moha**), (*v*) arrogance (**mada**) and (*vi*) envy (**matsara**). Krishnamurti has discussed all these tendencies found in all of us. They indicate immaturity, superficiality, lack of self-control and self-discipline. About greed, the sage has said the following:

"So long as the mind is seeking to be in a state of non-greed, surely it is still greedy." (24 : 84).

"We accept, we are gullible, we are greedy for new experiences. People swallow what is said by anybody with a beard, with promises, saying you will have a marvellous experience if you do certain things. ...So I have to understand my greed. What am I greedy for? Is it because I am fed up with this world, I have had women, I have had cars, I have had money and I want something more?" (14 : 23-24).

## 2-6 (83) IDENTIFICATION

Because most of us are not as important as we would like to be, and we have a feeling of dissatisfaction and inner emptiness, we get inclined to identify ourselves with the guru, some organisation, the nation, the tradition in order to have a feeling of belonging and to experience importance, power, recognition. We start liking the comfort derived from that. Krishnamurti has explained below how this happens through identification.

"This identification with something greater—the party, the country, the race, the religion, God—is the search for power. Because you yourself are empty, dull, weak, you like to identify yourself with something greater." (24 : 79).

"Identification with something is one of the most hypocritical states. To identify oneself with a nation, a belief, and yet remain alone is a favourite trick to cheat loneliness." (25 : 192).

"Identification, surely, is possession, the assertion of ownership; and ownership denies love. ...In identification there is resistance. ...Identification makes for insensitivity.

...Identification destroys freedom. ...Identification puts an end to discovery. It is another form of laziness. ...Identification is vicarious experience and, hence, utterly false. ...He who has identified himself can never know freedom in which alone all truth comes into being." (26 : 12-13).

## GROUP NO. 3

### 3-1 (76) HOLY

All of us who are brought up in a specific culture and tradition, consider a greater variety of objects holy, sacred, and have reverence and attachment to them. It may be a stone image, a metal idol, a book, a place, a building, or a river. It is believed to have divine properties and supernatural significance. It may appear rather strange, but what one person considers holy, sacred or divine, may not be so for another, and one may be quite insensitive, blind, to its holiness or divinity. Some persons are looked upon as holy, having divine powers, and phrases like 'his holiness' **sri sri**, **munishri**, are used before their names. But they are considered pious, holy, and the like only by a limited number of followers, not by all.

Krishnamurti has discussed the problem: what actually is holy, sacred? His answer to this question is very remarkable. It is mentioned in the following statements:

"All of us, at least those who are little serious and thoughtful and earnest, must have asked whether there is anything sacred at all, anything holy. Of course, the answer is that the temple, the mosque, the church is not holy, is not sacred, nor the images therein." (14 : 214).

"The image in a temple is no more holy than a piece of rock by the roadside. It is very important to find out what is really sacred, what is really holy if there is such a thing at all." (14 : 215).

"That which is holy, that which is sacred, which is truth, can only be when there is complete silence, when the brain itself has put thought in the right place. Out of that immense silence there is that which is sacred." (17 : 145).

## 3-2 (145) SACRED

The problem of what should be considered sacred and what should not is quite important, and not very easy to decide. It is clearly discussed by the sage in the following statements.

"A stone in a temple, an image in a church, a symbol is not sacred. Man calls them sacred, something holy, to be worshipped out of complicated urges, fears and longings. This 'sacredness' is still within the field of thought. ...In thought there is nothing new or holy. Thought can put together the intricacies of systems, dogmas, beliefs, and the symbols, images it projects are no more holy than the blueprints of a house or the design of a new aeroplane. ...There is nothing sacred or mystical about all this." (10 : 15).

"Is there anything sacred, holy? Obviously, the things which thought has put together in the religious sense—investing sacredness in images, in ideas—are not sacred at all." (17 : 197).

"There is that sacred thing, not in the things that man has put together, but which comes into being when man cuts himself off entirely from the past, which is memory ...that cessation of the past can only be when you see things as they are and come directly in contact with them." (14 : 216).

# GROUP NO. 4

## 4-1 (71) GRATIFICATION

Krishnamurti has differentiated clearly between happiness on one side and gratification, satisfaction and pleasure on the other. It is a very important difference which is usually overlooked by us. We are accustomed to like and prefer gratification. We take it mistakenly to be the same as happiness. We have considered pleasure separately in this same group. About gratification, Krishnamurti has said:

"We do not search out reality but go after gratification and sensation. It is essentially for self-glorification that we create the teacher, the master. ...If you are seeking gratification you will naturally find what you desire, but do not let us call it truth.

Truth comes into being when gratification, the desire for sensation, comes to an end." (26 : 117).

## 4-2 (75) HAPPINESS

Happiness is an important state of mind about which we often have a misconstrued notion. Krishnamurti has made this clear in several passages as follows:

"There is a difference between happiness and gratification. Happiness is a byproduct of something else. I am afraid most of us are seeking gratification. ...We want to find a sense of fullness at the end of our search." (24 : 9).

"Happiness comes uninvited; and the moment you are conscious that you are happy, you are no longer happy." (24 : 231).

The sage has brought out the intimate relation between truth and happiness thus:

"Truth or happiness cannot come without undertaking the journey into the ways of the self. You cannot travel far if you are anchored." (26 : 13).

"Truth must come; you cannot go to truth, and your cultivated virtue will not carry you to it. What you attain is not truth but your own self-projected desire; and in truth alone is there happiness." (26 : 13).

"Only when the mind is free from its own projections can there be happiness. Happiness that is bought is merely gratification. Happiness is not a remembrance; it is that state which comes into being with truth, ever new, never continuous." (27 : 71).

## 4-3 (133) PLEASURE

We crave for pleasure when we do not have it; we crave more when we have it to a limited extent. We go on seeking it in various ways, endlessly. Krishnamurti has brought out the important point that thinking is the factor that sustains pleasure, and it is necessary to understand thinking first, in order to deal with the problem of pleasure. Here are his words:

"It is thought that gives pleasure—as sexual pleasure and as the pleasure of achievement. Thought strengthens and gives continuity to pleasure of the moment. Thought, by thinking about that pleasure, gives it the vitality of the next moment of pleasure." (25 : 58).

"We need good, clean food... a clean floor to sleep on. ...But see what happens ...I must have it tomorrow. That means today's biological need has been made into tomorrow's pleasure, which is, thought has taken over. So, thinking is the factor one has to understand, not pleasure. ...So before you do anything with pleasure, before you nourish it, first find out what is thinking." (19 : 160).

## GROUP NO. 5

### 5-1 (11) BECOMING

Being and becoming are two states exclusive of each other. Becoming indicates desire for change. We are always desirous of a change, progress, improvement, the 'more'. This process of becoming has two sides, namely, 'I am **this**', and 'I want to be **that**'. The '**this**' is made by our own image of ourselves. The '**that**' is the goal projected, posited by our mind. Becoming many a time becomes an acute problem, causing much agony. Krishnamurti has pointed out that becoming causes conflict and prevents understanding. His statement is given below:

"To put aside the craving to be, to become, demands great intelligence and understanding. ...A mind burdened with becoming can never be tranquil, for tranquillity is not a result either of practice or of time. Tranquillity is a state of understanding and becoming denies this understanding. Becoming creates the sense of time, which is really the postponement of understanding. The 'I shall be' is an illusion born of self-importance." (26 : 22).

"As long as you want to become something, at whatever level, there is bound to be misery and confusion." (26 : 67).

### 5-2 (19) CELIBACY

Celibacy is **brahmacharya** in Sanskrit. In Yoga literature, it has come to be a very prestigious word. In the Hathayogapradīpikā of Swātmārāma (possibly 16th century A.D.), a practice called **vajroli mudrā** is described in detail. It involves sucking the semen back by the procedure of **nauli-madhyamā**, when there is ejaculation in a sexual act (III: 83-102). This technique is said to bestow upon the **yogin** emancipation (**muktidā**) even if he enjoys sexual pleasure (**bhogepi**) (III: 103). Of course, this does in no way apply to us, the common people. It may be true in the case of an individual who is the rarest of the rare. For most of us, **brahmacharya** is an impossibility. Krishnamurti has described celibacy in terms of a mind that understands the whole process of pleasure and fear. Here are his original words:

"What it means to be celibate has also been a problem for human beings, that also is part of life. Can the mind be completely chaste? Not being able to find out how to live a chaste life, one takes vows of celibacy and goes through tortures. That is not celibacy. Celibacy is something entirely different. It is to have a mind that is free from all images, from all knowledge; which means understanding the whole process of pleasure and fear." (14 : 82).

## 5-3 (40) DISCIPLINE

**See under 5-4 (50) EFFORT.**

## 5-4 (50) EFFORT

Effort is most essential in daily life. Effort including self-control, self-discipline, cultivating good habits, in connection with earning our livelihood, remaining fit and healthy, living our life actively, usefully, and shouldering our responsibilities efficiently, promptly, and adequately—effort in relation to all these states is a must. But this does not apply to effort in the spiritual, religious field. There, effort becomes a way of illusion, self-deception, a wild goose chase, because understanding, wisdom cannot be the result of effort, discipline, becoming. Krishnamurti has brought out this very significant, very remarkable point in the following statements. That is one of the most subtle truths, most outstanding contributions of the sage to human knowledge and wisdom.

"Our social, economic and so-called spiritual life is a series of efforts, always culminating in a certain result. And we think effort is essential, necessary. ...Very few of us realise that the self-centred activity of effort does not clear up any of the problems. On the contrary, it increases our confusion and our misery and our sorrow. ...We are constantly struggling to avoid facing **what is**, or we are trying to get away from it or to transform or modify **what is**." (24 : 42-43).

"Effort exists only as long as we are trying to avoid that inward loneliness, emptiness, but when we look at it, observe it, when we accept **what is** without avoidance, we will find there comes a state of being in which all strife ceases. That state of being is creativeness and it is not the result of strife." (24 : 45-46).

"It is only the wise, the extraordinarily intelligent, who are really free of effort, of struggle." (24 : 160).

## 5-5 (110) MIND MADE STILL

The human mind is unsteady by its very nature. To make it steady, still, many techniques and practices are recommended in yoga, and the experts of those practices are supposed to teach them to aspirants. Success in making the mind still is very hard to achieve. For this the practices are to be gone through for a pretty long time. This is supposed to be a highly specialised field of yoga, and the specialists demand a lot of money and respect. Krishnamurti has, however, shown very clearly the difference between a still mind and a mind made still. Here are two of his statements which must be remembered always.

"Obviously, the mind can be made still by the repetition of a word, of a chant, of a prayer. The mind can be drugged, put to sleep; it can be put to sleep pleasantly or violently, and during this sleep there may be dreams. But a mind that is made quiet by discipline, by ritual, by repetition, can never be alert, sensitive and free. This bludgeoning of the mind, subtly or crudely, is not meditation." (26 : 84).

"Stillness of the mind cannot be induced, it cannot be brought about through any practice or discipline. If the mind is **made** still, then whatever comes into it is only a self-projection, the response of memory. With the understanding of its conditioning, with the choiceless awareness of its own responses as thought and feeling, tranquillity comes to the mind." (27 : 80-81).

## 5-6 (134) PRACTICE

**See under 5-4 (50) EFFORT.**

## 5-7 (135) PRAYER

Prayer is a watchword of every religion. One seems to derive inner peace, assurance, support from it when we are under pressure of a calamity, when a situation becomes utterly hopeless, when the mind is overtaken by despair and terrible disappointment, when we are under the sway of profound grief. Prayer makes us hopeful about the future. Surrender, devotion, relying on divine help are its accompaniments. Religious authorities have always spoken in very high terms about prayer and its utility. But Krishnamurti has viewed prayer from an altogether different angle, giving more importance to 'discover the truth of **what is**'. Here is his original statement:

"When you feel all alone, when you are depressed and in sorrow, you ask God for help; so what you call prayer is a petition. The form of prayer may vary, but the intent behind it is generally the same. Prayer with most people is a petition, a begging, an asking ...The real thing is to understand yourself, to see why you are perpetually asking for something, why there is in you this demand, this urge to beg. The more you know yourself through awareness of what you are thinking, what you are feeling, the more you will discover the truth of **what is**; and it is truth that will help you to be free." (24 : 182).

## 5-8 (141) RELIGION

The human mind has engaged itself in religion, philosophy and rules of ethical conduct throughout the world for the last three thousand years or more. These inquiries purport to fill man's life with virtue, discipline, order, peace and happiness and teach him how to live and work for the good of all at all times. But this goal seems always to have eluded man. That is because good has not always prevailed over evil. Krishnamurti has dealt with the problems of what religion is, what it is not, what it does, and how it is supposed to do it, in the following statements:

"Do you know what religion is? It is not in the chant, it is not in the performance of any ritual, it is not in the worship of tin gods or stone images. It is not in the temples and churches, it is not in the reading of the Bible or the Gita, it is not in the repeating of a sacred name or in the following of some other superstition invented by man. None of this is religion. Religion is the feeling of goodness, of that love which is like the river, living, moving, everlastingly. In that state, you will find there comes a moment when there is no longer any search at all." (24 : 144-145).

"A religious man is not really one who puts on a robe or a loincloth, or lives on one meal a day, or has taken innumerable vows to be **this**, and not to be **that**, but who is inwardly simple, who is not becoming anything." (24 : 65-66).

## 5-9 (142) RENUNCIATION

To renounce means to give up. We usually renounce something in order to gain or possess a higher, more important or more pleasurable thing, state, or position. Renunciation is called **vairāgya** or **virāga** in Sanskrit. It is given supreme importance in yoga as a means to achieve the goal of emancipation (**kaivalya**). Two grades of **vairāgya**, the lower and the higher, are recognised.

Krishnamurti has pointed out that, "there is renunciation only when there is no gain in the act of renouncing". (10 : 111). This is called '**para-vairāgya**' in the Yogasūtra of Patanjali (I : 16). The lower **vairāgya** is defined in **sūtra** I : 15. Krishnamurti looks upon renunciation as giving up worldliness, and being free from inner complexities, cultivation of virtue, fear, wants, and beliefs. This is an extremely important point of view, which he has explained in the following statements:

"What you are renouncing is the society of men, but not the things which man has made out of the world. You are not renouncing the culture, the tradition, the knowledge all of that goes with you when you withdraw from the world. ...The sannyāsis and saints are violent in their controls and demands. So essentially, though they may put on the saffron robe or the black robe they are all very worldly." (25 : 44-45).

A very important quality of an aspirant who renounces the world is mentioned by the sage thus:

"The sannyasi who outwardly lives very simply may be inwardly very complex, cultivating virtue, wanting to attain truth, God. What is important is to be inwardly very simple, very austere, which is to have a mind not clogged with beliefs, with fears, with innumerable wants, for only such a mind is capable of real thinking, of exploration and discovery." (29 : 68).

## 5-10 (144) RITUAL

Rituals form an important part of religion. They provide a welcome change from the monotonous routine of daily life. They have an appeal to the common people because they are based on the beliefs which the common people usually entertain. Krishnamurti looks upon them as a vain activity and points out that they come in the way of self-knowledge, which is the really important, first thing that one must have. His own words are reproduced below:

"Obviously, rituals offer to the participants an atmosphere in which they feel good. Both collective and individual rituals give a certain quietness to the mind; they offer a vital contrast to the everyday humdrum life. There is a certain amount of beauty and orderliness in ceremonies, but fundamentally they are stimulants; and as with all stimulants, they soon dull the mind and heart. Rituals become a habit; they become a necessity, and one cannot do without them. ...Rituals are a vain repetition which offer a marvellous and respectable escape from self-knowledge. Without self-knowledge, action has very little significance." (26 : 241).

## 5-11 (180) VIRTUE

Virtue means morally commendable, morally essential qualities which together constitute chastity. Being virtuous and practising virtue are two very different things. Krishnamurti gives due importance to the former, but not to the latter. He equates practising non-violence and truthfulness with the absence of these two qualities, and points out that cultivation of them, trying to adopt them, imbibe them is a vain pursuit. This is a very significant truth, and although it goes against the prestigious practices of Yoga called the **yama-niyamas** (abstinences and observances), it must be understood clearly and carefully. Here are the original words of the sage:

"Virtue is essential, for it gives freedom. It is only in virtue that you can discover, that you can live—not in the **cultivation** of virtue, which merely brings about respectability. There is a difference between being virtuous and becoming virtuous. Being virtuous comes through the understanding of **what is**, whereas becoming virtuous is postponement, the covering up of **what is** with what you would like to be." (24 : 23-24).

"Being virtuous has very little meaning in itself; but because you are virtuous, there is precision in your thought, order in your whole being, and that is the function of virtue." (24 : 119).

"Virtue gives freedom; but cultivated humility is not virtue. It is mere sensation and, therefore, harmful and destructive; it is a bondage, to be broken again and again." (26 : 66).

## 5-12 (186) WORSHIP

Worship is called **bhakti** or **poojā** in Sanskrit. The worshipper is called a **bhakta**. Credulousness, devotion and gullibility are prominent constituents of worship. A very large majority of any population is formed by **bhaktas**. Worship is a very widespread tendency of human beings. The objects worshipped are: God, scriptures, saints, success, and those who are in power. Krishnamurti has clearly pointed out the weak and unfavourable aspects of worship. He has said:

"The worshipper is the worshipped. To worship another is to worship oneself. The image, the symbol, is the projection of oneself. After all, your idol, your book, your prayer is the reflection of your background; it is your creation, though it be made by another. You choose according to your gratification; your choice is your prejudice. Your image is your intoxicant, and it is carved out of your own memory; you are worshipping yourself through the image created by your own thought. ... Such devotion is a form of self-deception." (27 : 40).

"As long as there is fear, you live in darkness. Your worship is out of that darkness and, therefore, worship is absolutely meaningless." (15 : 9).

## GROUP NO. 6

### 6-1 (13) BENEDICTION

Benediction means a divine blessing. Krishnamurti has used this word for his own inner state of silence, innocence, meditation, stillness, simplicity, austerity and love. He has described that state at some places in his writings. Here are two examples:

"Only on waking early next morning, one was aware of the previous evening's splendour and the love that went by. Consciousness cannot contain the immensity of innocence. ...The entire consciousness must be still, not wanting, not seeking and never pursuing. ...Meditation is the emptying of consciousness. ...There must be space for stillness, not the space created by thought and its activities but that space that comes through denial and destruction, when there is nothing left of thought and its projection. In emptiness alone can there be creation. ...Several times during the day, at odd moments, that benediction would come and pass away. Desiring and asking have no significance whatsoever." (10 : 51).

"That strange benediction comes when it will, but with each visitation, deep within, there is a transformation; it is never the same." (10 : 53).

### 6-2 (14) BLISS

Bliss is also a state like benediction, full of peace, innocence, understanding, discovery, observation, listening. This is how the sage has described it:

"It is only when the mind transcends time that truth ceases to be an abstraction. Then bliss is not an idea derived from pleasure but an actuality that is not verbal." (25 : 132).

"Meditation is the awakening of bliss. ...Thought is like the smoke of a fire and bliss is the fire without the cloud of smoke. ...Pleasure is one thing and bliss another. ...This bliss comes out of complete silence." (25 : 134).

## 6-3 (68) FRESH MIND

A fresh mind is not influenced by the past, which has freedom from the known, aloneness, self-knowledge and self-abandonment. It can deal with the problems of human life directly, simply. Krishnamurti has explained it as follows:

"We all ought to wash our minds completely clean, as the trees are washed by the rain, because they are so heavily laden with the dust of many centuries, the dust of what we call knowledge, experience. If you and I would clean the mind everyday, free it of yesterday's reminiscences, each one of us would then have a fresh mind, a mind capable of dealing with the many problems of existence." (24 : 137).

"When the mind renews itself without forming new patterns, habits, without again falling into the groove of limitation, then it remains fresh, young, innocent, and is therefore capable of infinite understanding. For such a mind there is no death, because there is no longer a process of accumulation." (24 : 141).

## 6-4 (95) JOY

Joy is a state of mind which we all wish to be in. But it is necessary to know the difference between joy and pleasure. Krishnamurti has pointed out that pleasure and fear are interrelated and that joy is there when desire is absent. Here are his own words:

"Thought nourishes pleasure—which has nothing whatever to do with joy. Joy is not the product of thought. It is not pleasure. You can cultivate pleasure, you can think about it endlessly; you cannot do that with joy." (6 : 67).

"If you can look at all things ...without wanting the experience to be repeated, then there will be no pain, no fear, and, therefore, tremendous joy. It is the struggle to repeat and perpetuate pleasure which turns it into pain." (21 : 37).

## 6-5 (115) NEW

**See under 13-3 (34) CREATIVENESS.**

# GROUP NO. 7

## 7-1 (69) GOALS

**See under 7-3 (82) IDEALS.**

## 7-2 (81) IDEA

Human beings are endowed with the capacity to think, to form ideas from the revival of traces of past experiences stored in the brain cells. Memory traces are conditioned by previous experience. This is a necessary process built up in the formation of those traces. Krishnamurti has emphasised the fact that ideas do not and cannot make for truth or understanding. Here are his actual words:

"As our society is mostly constructed on the intellectual or verbal level, the idea comes first with all of us and action follows. ...When action is compelled by an idea, action can never liberate man. It is extraordinarily important for us to understand this point." (24 : 30-31).

"Only when one can go beyond the bundle of ideas—which is the 'me', which is the mind, which has a partial or complete continuity—only when one can go beyond that, when thought is completely silent, is there a state of experiencing. Then one shall know what truth is." (24 : 34).

"Ideas are not truth, and truth is something that must be experienced directly, from moment to moment." (24 : 34).

## 7-3 (82) IDEALS

In our life we often entertain ideas about a change in our situation, about being different from what we think, we are. In this process of becoming, we project an ideal, a state which is far away, which is to be reached as a result of much effort and strife, under the guidance of an expert, a guru, an authority. Krishnamurti has pointed out the basic fact about such ideals that, howsoever high, noble, desirable and commendable an ideal may appear to be, it is a reaction to **what is**. It is projected by an uneasy, miserable mind, and that it never contains any truth. His words are reproduced below:

"All opposites are self-projected; the ideal is a reaction from **what is**, and the conflict to achieve the ideal is a vain and illusory struggle within the cage of thought. Through this conflict there is no release, no freedom for man." (27 : 33).

"It is the ideal that creates the opposite to **what is**, so if you know how to be with **what is**, then the opposite is not necessary. Trying to become like somebody else or like your ideal is one of the main causes of contradiction, confusion and conflict. A mind that is confused, whatever it does, at any level, will remain confused." (21 : 66).

"You need have no ideals. On the contrary, ideals prevent immediate understanding. We are fed on illusions, on things that have no value, and we easily succumb to authority, to religious as well as political tyranny; and how can such a mind discover that which is eternal, that which is beyond the projections of itself?" (18 : 6).

## 7-4 (86) IMAGE

The word 'image' is an important word in Krishnamurti's vocabulary. The human mind has ideas, notions, assumptions, opinions, conclusions, beliefs, about oneself and about the objects, things, happenings, and events that form our experience. For them Krishnamurti uses the word 'image' or the 'me', or the 'centre' the 'observer' or the 'thinker'. Having images is a very special quality of the human mind. We form images and use them all the time, but we are hardly ever aware of their existence in our minds. If we can give our total attention to them and be aware of the mechanism of their formation, then they come to an end. Thereby a great hurdle in understanding, in seeing, in looking, is removed, and there is direct perception of anything. Here is an account of how this happens in the words of the sage:

"Images are formed when the mind is not attentive, and most of our minds are inattentive. When you are aware of one image attentively, and you are also attentively aware of the whole mechanism of building of images and how it operates, then in that attention the building of all images comes to an end; whether they be of the past, the present or the future. What matters is the state of attention, not how many images you have. Do please try and understand this, because it is most important. If you can really grasp this, then you have understood completely all the machinery of the mind." (14 : 338).

"Please do understand this very simple fact that we not only look at nature with the eyes that have accumulated knowledge about nature and, therefore, with an image, but we also look at human beings with our various forms of conclusions, opinions, judgements and values. ...So when you look, when you observe your life, you observe through the image, through the conclusions you have already formed. ...Therefore you are not actually looking at life. Do you understand this very simple fact?" (13 : 4).

"So that is the first thing: to observe without the observer, ...without the image. ...You have to find out how to look at the image that you have created about yourself outwardly, the symbol, and also to look deeply within yourself." (6 : 20).

"It is only when the image is not there that you can see completely. The image is the observer, is the centre from which you observe." (20 : 84).

## 7-5 (113) NAMING

The human brain makes use of words as symbols for objects, actions, qualities, and happenings, and thereby it has come to have a marvellous power to express sensations, feelings, and experiences. This involves the process of naming, which is the process of association between linguistic and non-linguistic events. It is one of the most wonderful examples of the phenomenon of habit-formation. The word can be stored and revived in the brain and associated with a sensation very easily, and the mind can move from object to object, experience to experience very swiftly with the help of words, i.e., naming. Naming has resulted in two dangerous consequences for the human mind. It has taken away the possibility of stillness, silence of the mind, and it has helped the development, the coming into existence of the 'me' or the self, which is a fictitious entity. Krishnamurti has considered naming in relation to its influence on the 'me'. He has said:

"Why has naming become so important? I name my house, my wife, my child. Naming strengthens the 'me'. If I did not name, what would happen? Anger would be over." (19 : 137).

"Our whole consciousness is a process of naming or terming experience, and then storing or recording it. It is this process that gives nourishment and strength to the illusory entity, the experiencer as distinct and separate from the experience." (26 : 69).

"The mind can be still only when it is not experiencing, i.e., when it is not terming or naming, recording or storing up in memory. This naming and recording is a constant process of the different layers of consciousness." (26 : 44).

## 7-6 (166) SYMBOLS

Words, images, figures, and some objects like birds, animals, the flag, are used by man as symbols. They are associated with particular feelings, reactions and emotions and have great significance for national, social life, or for the whole of humanity. Krishnamurti has brought out the following facts about symbols:

"Symbols are a device of the brain to protect the psyche; this is the whole process of thought. The 'me' is a symbol, not an actuality." (25 : 268).

"Mere words have an extraordinary significance for us. They have a neurological effect whose sensations are more important than what is beyond the symbol. The symbol, the image, the flag, the sound are all important; substitution and not reality is our strength." (26 : 62).

## 7-7 (185) WORDS

**See under 7-5 (113) NAMING, and under 7-6 (166) SYMBOLS.**

## GROUP NO. 8

### 8-1 (107) MEDITATION

The word 'meditation' indicates two different states which have no relation with each other. This is a fact which very few of us are aware of, and that has given rise to a lot of confusion. Most of us, who are not well-informed, take meditation to be a state of concentration of the mind on one object to the exclusion of all other objects. In the Yogasūtra of Patanjali, this state of concentration is called **dhāranā, dhyāna**, or **sabeeja samādhi**, depending upon the intensity of absorption of the mind into the object of concentration. (III : 1-4). The other meaning of the word 'meditation', which Krishnamurti has emphasised, is 'a state of enlightenment'. It is called by various names, such as, '**Dharmamegha-samādhi**', '**Nirbeeja-samādhi**', '**Sahajāvasthā**' or '**Jeevan-mukti**'. This state is wholly different from meditation in the former sense. This difference is very crucial, and we are usually totally unaware of this fact. Krishnamurti has brought out clearly this crucial difference in many of his statements.

"It is one of the favourite sayings of the meditator or the teacher who practises or teaches meditation that people must learn concentration—that is to concentrate on one thought, drive out every other thought and fix your mind on that one thought only. This is a most stupid thing to do. ...When you do that you are merely resisting, you are having a battle between the demand that you must concentrate on one thing and your mind wandering to all kinds of other things." (20 : 84).

"You can never say that you are meditating or set aside a period for meditation. It isn't at your command. Its benediction doesn't come to you because you lead a systematised life or follow a particular routine or morality. It comes only when your heart is really open. ...It comes without your knowing, without your invitation. But you can never guard it, keep it, worship it. If you try, it will never come again; do what you will, it will avoid you." (25 : 82).

"Meditation is not the repetitive formula of **mantras**, of breathing rhythmically, of sitting in a certain posture, practising awareness, practising attention—these are all utterly mechanical. ...And you have practised these mechanical things for centuries upon centuries." (20 : 83).

"A mind that is capable of concentration is not necessarily able to meditate. Self-interest does bring about concentration, like any other interest, but such concentration implies a motive, a cause, conscious or unconscious; there is always a thing to be gained or set aside, an effort to comprehend, to get to the other shore. Attention with an aim is concerned with accumulation. The attention that comes with this movement towards or away from something is the attraction of pleasure or the repulsion of pain, but meditation is that extraordinary attention in which there is no maker of effort, no end or object to be gained. Effort is part of the acquisitive process, it is the gathering of experience by the experiencer. ...There is great bliss in meditation." (27 : 219).

## 8-2 (137) QUIET MIND

A quiet mind is a necessary pre-requisite for understanding anything clearly. If the mind is unsteady, there can be only partial attention and so, no understanding. This fact has been brought out very clearly and repeatedly by the sage. But we cannot usually benefit from this important finding because our minds are always unsteady and wandering from desire to desire and thus from distraction to distraction. Here are the original words of the sage:

"To understand any of these problems we have to have a very quiet mind, a very still mind, so that the mind can look at the problem without interposing ideas or theories, without any distraction." (24 : 85).

"There is understanding only when the mind is quiet, and the mind is not quiet when it is held in an ideology, dogma or belief or when it is bound to the pattern of its own experiences, memories. The mind is not quiet when it is acquiring or becoming. ...The mind is quiet only when it is not caught in thought which is the net of its own activity. When the mind is still, not **made** still, a true factor, love comes into being." (27 : 31-32).

"When the mind is quiet, it can see and hear much more, see things as they are—not invent, not imagine," (14 : 445).

## 8-3 (159) SILENCE

**See under 8-4 (163) SPACE.**

## 8-4 (163) SPACE

The three words, space, spaciousness, and emptiness indicate the absence of all mental activity like desire, memory, thought and emotions. That makes for undistracted attention, seeing, direct perception and understanding. Krishnamurti has described this fact in the following passages:

"Silence demands space, space in the whole structure of consciousness. There is no space in the structure of one's consciousness as it is, because it is crowded with fears—crowded, chattering, chattering. When there is silence, there is immense, timeless space; then only is there a possibility of coming upon that which is the eternal, sacred." (17 : 145).

"There must be space for stillness, not the space created by thought and its activities but that space that comes through denial and destruction, when there is nothing left of thought and its projection. In emptiness alone can there be creation." (10 : 51).

"If your mind has space, then in that space there is silence—and from that silence everything else comes, for then you can listen, you can pay attention without resistance. That is why it is important to have space in the mind." (29 : 135).

"Silence and spaciousness go together. The immensity of silence is the immensity of the mind in which a centre does not exist." (25 : 38).

"It is only when the mind is completely still... that there is harmony, there is vast space and silence." (14 : 375).

## 8-5 (165) STILLNESS

**See under 8-4 (163) SPACE.**

## 8-6 (173) TRANQUILLITY

**See under 8-4 (163) SPACE.**

# GROUP NO. 9

## 9-1 (119) OBSERVED

Among the illusions entertained by the human mind, the most widespread is that about the separate existence of the 'I', the 'me', the self, the observer, the thinker, or the experiencer, apart from that which is observed, seen, thought of, or experienced. Krishnamurti tried throughout his life to make us aware of the illusory nature of the observer, the 'me', but due to our very strong habit of thinking, imagining, that unless there is an observer, a thinker, already, how can there be that which is observed, the thought? The two of them must be in existence independently of each other—due to this habit, the truth brought out by the sage has always eluded us, and we find it very difficult to realise it in our experience of the world. Let us see how the sage has explained this basic fact in various statements.

"This is very important to understand. We have separated the thing observed from the observer and from this arises not only the problem of interpretation but also conflict, and the many problems connected with it. This division is an illusion." (25 : 269).

"The phenomenon of the observer and the observed is not a dual process, but a single one; and only in experiencing the fact of this unitary process is there freedom from desire, from conflict." (26 : 61).

"The fact is, there is no duality and the observer is the observed at all times." (19 : 58).

"When you actually see and test by observing that the observer and the observed are actually one, then you end all conflict in life, in all relationships." (6 : 56).

## 9-2 (138) REALITY

Krishnamurti often used the phrase **what is** for truth, reality. But he never entertained the idea of ultimate reality or absolute truth like **brahman** or **ātman**. Reality, for him, was not something permanent, static, or unchanging (**aparināmi**). On the contrary, he regarded it as ever new, from moment to moment. It is very important to understand this view very clearly, because many of us are traditionally inclined to believe in the existence of a permanent, ultimate, absolute, unchanging reality as the fundamental basis of the universe.

"Reality has no continuity; it is from moment to moment, ever new, ever fresh. What has continuity can never be creative. ...Reality is not to be spoken of; and when it is, it is no longer reality." (26 : 45).

"There is a reality which, coming upon the mind, transforms it. You don't have to do a thing. ...A mind that is seeking it will never find it; but there is that state unquestionably... You cannot come to it through any means, through any book, through any guru or organisation." (18 : 2).

"When the mind is utterly still, only then is there freedom for the real to be." (27 : 7).

## 9-3 (175) TRUTH

**See under Mahāvākya No. 5, Chapter 2.**

## 9-4 (178) UNKNOWN

**See under 14-4 (96) KNOWING ONESELF.**

## 9-5 (182) WHAT IS

This is a peculiar phrase appearing in the talks of J. Krishnamurti quite often. It means what the situation actually is, i.e., truth or reality. It can be understood through direct perception only by a still, silent mind, which can give total attention. This is what the sage has said about it:

"To understand **what is** one must observe what one thinks, feels and does from moment to moment. That is the actual. ...To understand **what is** requires a state of mind in which there is no identification or condemnation, which means a mind that is alert and yet passive. We are in that state when we really desire to understand something; when the intensity of interest is there, that state of mind comes into being." (24 : 25).

"The **what is** is to be seen in the mirror of relationship, relationship with all things. The **what is** cannot be understood in withdrawal, in isolation; it cannot be understood if there is the interpreter, the translator who denies or accepts. The **what is** can be understood only when the mind is passive. ...It is extremely difficult as long as there is thought." (27 : 63).

## GROUP NO. 10

### 10-1 (39) DIRECT PERCEPTION

**See under 10-4 (61) EXPERIENCING.**

### 10-2 (41) DISCOVERY

**See under 10-4 (61) EXPERIENCING.**

### 10-3 (57) ENLIGHTENMENT

**See under 10-4 (61) EXPERIENCING.**

### 10-4 (61) EXPERIENCING

Krishnamurti has pointed out the fact that there is vast difference between experience and experiencing. The former is accompanied by sensation, memory, thought, naming, and desire. Experiencing, on the other hand, precludes all such associations. It is direct perception. There is total attention and passive awareness in experiencing. Krishnamurti has used other words like perception, discovery, enlightenment, for experiencing. Here are some of his own statements:

"Experiencing is not sensation. ...The actual, the **what is**, cannot be understood through mere sensation. The senses play a limited part, but understanding or experiencing lies beyond and above the senses. Sensation becomes important only when experiencing ceases, then words are significant and symbols dominate." (26 : 62).

"The mind is empty only when thought is not. ...In experiencing there is neither the experiencer nor the experienced. The experienced is the thought, which gives birth to the thinker. Only when the mind is experiencing is there stillness, the silence which is not made up, put together; and only in that tranquillity can the real come into being. Reality is not of time and is not measurable." (27 : 27).

"There can be a direct experiencing, that is, experiencing without the observer. Then only is there a possibility of being completely open, of being as nothing, and then there is the perception of the real." (18 : 20).

"Enlightenment does not come through a leader or through a teacher; it comes through the understanding of **what is** in yourself—not going away from yourself. The mind has to understand actually what is going on in its psychological field." (6 : 89).

## 10-5 (62) FALSE AS THE FALSE

Truth and falsehood are both part of human life. Truth is desired by all of us, and we always want to avoid, to remain free from, what is false. This is because truth makes us successful, while falsehood causes failure. We have noted earlier, in Chapter No. 2, a **mahāvākya** of J. Krishnamurti, namely, that 'negation is the most positive action'. For the establishment of order, it is necessary to understand disorder, and that understanding itself makes for order. In the same way, seeing the false as the false is, in itself, the establishment of truth. We are usually not aware of this important fact pointed out by the sage and we feel with great confidence that positive action is a must for coming upon truth. Understanding the false means freedom from the false, which, in itself, is the truth. Let us see how the sage has brought out this crucial fact:

"When you see that the false is the false, it gives you tremendous energy and freedom to see the truth as the truth, not as an illusion or fancy of the mind." (25 : 152).

"The understanding of the actual is possible only when the ideal, the **what should be** is erased from the mind, that is, only when the false is seen as the false. The **what should be** is also the **what should not be**." (27 : 84).

"The perception of the false as the false is the ending of the false." (28 : 8).

## 10-6 (89) INSIGHT

Insight means understanding all details and the underlying factors and situations. Krishnamurti has used several other words as having almost the same meaning as insight, for example, direct perception, total attention, passive awareness, discovery, and intelligence. To use some other phrases peculiar to Krishnamurti's exposition, we may say that insight comes into being with the ending of thought, freedom from the known, or dying to the past. It means coming face to face with reality, truth, or **what is**. Krishnamurti has explained 'insight' as follows:

"Insight is not an act of remembrance, the continuation of memory. Insight is like a flash of light. You see with absolute clarity, all the complications, the consequences, the intricacies. Then this very insight is action, complete. ...This is pure, clear insight—perception without any shadow of doubt." (11 : 73).

"That insight is outside the brain. ...That insight and its action changes the very brain cells. ...This whole movement from watching, listening to the thunder of insight is one movement; it is not coming to it step by step. It is like a swift arrow, and that insight can alone uncondition the brain. ...When there is an ending to thought and to time, there is total insight. Only then can there be the flowering of the brain." (11 : 74).

## 10-7 (118) OBSERVATION

Observation means paying attention. But we usually do not pay, we cannot pay full, total attention, because our mind is being pulled in various directions due to the cravings present in it. This constitutes distraction, and makes for lack of understanding, illusion, and self-deception. Krishnamurti has pointed out the importance of observing without the observer. This is a very special, very significant finding of the sage. This is how he has described it:

"There is a vast difference between observation and experience. In observation there is no observer at all, there is only observing. There is not the one who observes and is divided off from the thing observed." (6 : 89).

**Also see under 17-6 (103) LOOKING.**

## 10-8 (131) PERCEPTION

**See under 17-6 (103) LOOKING.**

# GROUP NO. 11

## 11-1 (20) CENTRE

In Krishnamurti's terminology, the word 'centre' is used for the 'me' or self. In human beings, it is absent at birth, but develops in the inter-relationship with the surroundings, and once developed, around the age of three years, it works throughout life as the foundation of the feeling and experience of one's separate existence as a human being. In animals, it may be said that there is only a rudimentary 'I' or 'me', which is essential just for survival. For further information, **see under Mahāvākya No. 12, Chapter 2**.

## 11-2 (52) ENDING OF SELF

The self is a fictitious entity, an illusion, at one level. But at the level of daily life, in one's relationship with the world around, self-awareness or ego feeling is quite essential for being able to live as a separate, individual human being. It is developed by one's name, one's desires, one's limitations, qualities, abilities, capacities, and so on. This part of the self is essential. It is not illusory. Without it human life would be hardly different from animal life. The illusory part is made by the dual feeling or projection of the mind, 'I am this' and 'I want to be that' or 'I want to have that'. This is fictitious, not essential, and it can be put to an end. How this ending comes about is explained by the sage as follows:

"The self hides in many garments, in many structures; it varies from time to time, but there is always this self, this separative, self-centred activity which imagines that one day it will make itself something which it is not. ...There is only the ending of all that, and that ending does not require time. ...Remembrances, however pleasurable, have no reality, they are things of the past, gone, finished, dead." (11 : 41).

"Where the self ends, with all its secret and open intrigues, its compulsive urges and demands, its joys and sorrows, there begins a movement of life that is beyond time and its bondage." (10 : 118).

## 11-3 (60) EXPERIENCER

**See under Mahāvākya No. 12, Chapter 2.**

## 11-4 (106) ME

The sage has described the 'me' very clearly in the following passage:

"Surely, the 'me' is the result of our education, of our conflicts, of our culture, of our relationship with the rest of the world. That 'me' is the result of the propaganda which we have been subjected to for five thousand years. ...It is that 'me' which says, 'I want to be happy', 'I must be successful', 'I have achieved'. ...Only with the ending of the 'me' is there passion." (14 : 340).

## 11-5 (120) OBSERVER

## 11-6 (153) SELF

## 11-7 (167) THINKER

**See all the above categories under Mahāvākya No. 12, Chapter 2.**

# GROUP NO. 12

## 12-1 (15) BODY

The body and mind are our two natural endowments which we use throughout life. Krishnamurti dealt with the human mind in all its aspects, including conditioning, fear, desire, illusion, as well as enlightenment, understanding and wisdom. He was not unaware of the importance of keeping the body fit and healthy. Throughout his long life of 91 years, he was very particular about the upkeep and proper maintenance of the body. He has all through given much importance to the harmonious inter-relationship between the body and the brain. He has said about the body:

"Most of us are not sensitive even physically. We overeat, we do not bother about the right diet. ...Our bodies become gross and insensitive; the quality of attention in the organism itself is made dull. How can there be a very alert, sensitive, clear mind if the organism itself is dull and heavy?" (21 : 23).

"A fat, gross body does interfere with the subtleties of thought, and thought escaping from the conflicts and problems it has bred does make the body a perverse thing. ...When the absolute necessity of the complete harmony of the brain and body is seen, then the brain will watch over the body, not dominating it, and this very watching sharpens the brain and makes the body sensitive. The seeing is the fact and with the fact there is no bargaining." (10 : 130).

"The body must be extraordinarily sensitive. ...The body affects the mind and the mind affects the body, and for this reason, sensitivity of the body, the organism, is essential." (6 : 50).

## GROUP NO. 13

### 13-1 (4) ANONYMITY

Most of us crave importance, recognition, praise, flattery, excellence, fame. Actually that is a sign of being immature, superficial and full of vanity. But it is a very widespread tendency of human beings to crave popularity. A person of wisdom, insight, understanding, however, prefers to go unnoticed, without much attention. This attitude of being anonymous is given various names by Krishnamurti, such as austerity, humility, innocence, sensitiveness, or simplicity. All these characteristics have much in common. About anonymity he has said:

"Anonymity is humility; it does not lie in the change of name, cloth, or with the identification with that which may be anonymous, an ideal, a heroic act, country and so on. Anonymity is an act of the brain, the conscious anonymity. There is an anonymity which comes with the awareness of the complete.

The complete is never within the field of the brain or idea." (10 : 10).

"Austerity is the summation of intelligence. This austerity can be only when there is self-abandonment, and it cannot be through will, through choice, through deliberate interest." (25 : 41).

"Austerity does not lie in any outward symbol or act: wearing a loincloth or a monk's robe, taking only one meal a day, or living the life of a hermit. Such disciplined simplicity, however rigorous, is not austerity; it is merely an outward show without an inner reality. Austerity is the simplicity of inward aloneness, the simplicity of a mind that is purged of all conflict, that is not caught in the fire of desire, even the desire for the highest." (28 : 23).

"That insecurity which comes from the flowering of security is humility and innocence whose strength the arrogant can never know." (10 : 208).

"You can't be vulnerable without innocence, and though you have a thousand experiences, a thousand smiles and tears, if you don't die to them, how can the mind be innocent? It is only the innocent mind—in spite of its thousand experiences—that can see what truth is." (25 : 85).

"Only the innocent mind can inquire into the unknown. But the calculated innocence, which may wear a loincloth or the robe of a monk, is not that passion of self-abandonment from which come courtesy, gentleness, humility, patience—the expressions of love." (12 : 21-22).

"We can abandon ourselves only when there is austerity, a sense of great inward simplicity. ...But that state can come into being only when the mind is no longer thinking in terms of 'the more', in terms of having or becoming something through time." (24 : 130).

"From this deep self-abandonment... the whole structure of the mind becomes quiet. It is really a state of pure attention and out of this comes a bliss, an ecstacy, that cannot be put into words." (25 : 50).

"Without being simple one cannot be sensitive—to the trees, to the birds, to the mountains, to the wind, to all the things which are going on about us in the world." (24 : 65).

"Sensitivity is wholly different from refinement; sensitivity is an integral state, refinement is always partial. ...Only the sensitive can face the actual, without escaping into all kinds of conclusions, opinions, and accumulations." (10 : 151).

"To be simple in the whole, total process of our consciousness is extremely arduous. ...It means to be aware of our fears, of our hopes, and to investigate and to be free of them more and more and more." (24 : 65).

"Simplicity and sincerity can never be companions. He who is identified with something, at whatever level, may be sincere but he is not simple. The will to be is the very antithesis of simplicity. Simplicity comes into being with freedom from the acquisitive drive of the desire to achieve." (26 : 80).

Under this article on anonymity 13-1 (4), we have included other problems of life which are very intimately related to it, namely, austerity, humility, innocence, self-abandonment, sensitiveness and simplicity. Krishnamurti's statements on all these are grouped together here.

## 13-2 (8) AUSTERITY

**See under 13-1 (4) ANONYMITY.**

## 13-3 (34) CREATIVENESS

Creativeness, creativity or 'the new' is a very remarkable feature of the world brought out by the sage in his discourses. We are always under the influence of the past, the known, the familiar. So our relationship is a movement from the known to the known, never to the 'new', to the unknown. And we are deprived of creative happiness, the joy of 'being'. This is explained by Krishnamurti in the following statements:

"The 'new' is never a sensation; therefore, it can never be recognised, re-experienced. It is a state of being in which creativeness comes, without invitation, without memory, and that is reality." (24 : 76).

"Only the mind which has no walls, no foothold, no barrier, no resting place, which is moving completely with life, timelessly, pushing on, exploring, exploding—only such a mind can be happy, eternally new, because it is creative in itself." (24 : 144).

"Extraordinary creativeness comes with the discovery of what is true. Unfortunately, most of us do not know this creativeness because we have burdened our minds with knowledge, tradition, memory, with what Shankara, Buddha, Marx or some other person has said." (24 : 148).

"You and I have intrinsically the capacity to be happy, to be creative, to be in touch with something that is beyond the clutches of time. Creative happiness is not a gift reserved for the few. ...Creative happiness has no value in the market. It is not a commodity to be sold to the highest bidder, but it is the one thing that can be for all." (27 : 2).

"Creativeness is not a process of becoming or achieving, but a state of being in which self-seeking effort is totally absent. When the self makes an effort to be absent, the self is present. All effort on the part of the complex thing called the mind must cease without any motive or inducement." (28 : 70).

## 13-4 (79) HUMILITY

**See under 13-1 (4) ANONYMITY.**

## 13-5 (88) INNOCENCE

**See under 13-1 (4) ANONYMITY.**

## 13-6 (116) NOTHINGNESS

The fact that human life, human achievements actually form a very insignificant, negligible, unimportant part of the universe and man has very little value in the whole scheme of the universe—this fact was known very well by our ancients. We agree with it when the mind is filled with despair when a great calamity befalls us. But otherwise we are always inclined to boast of our skills, knowledge and capacities. Krishnamurti has drawn attention to the fact that it is very important to be aware of our being 'as nothing' in the world, in our life. Here are his own words:

"To be as nothing is essential. ...You can look at it very simply. ...If we can... merely silently observe the process of desire, which is oneself... then only is there a possibility of being completely open, of being as nothing, and then there is the reception of the real." (18 : 18-20).

"It is this fear of being nothing that drives the self into activity; but it **is** nothing. It is an emptiness. If we are able to face that emptiness, to be with that aching loneliness, then fear altogether disappears and a fundamental transformation takes place. For this to happen, there must be the experiencing of that nothingness. ...It is the experiencing of **what is** without naming it that brings about freedom from **what is**." (26 : 54).

## 13-7 (117) NOW

We are all trained to believe by tradition that the state of ultimate truth or absolute reality, which is an eternal, timeless state, can be achieved only through a long drawn-out spiritual effort. This is a belief which Krishnamurti has shown to be hollow and false. He lays emphasis on the 'now'. His point, although it is very significant, is not easy to understand. His own words are as follows:

"Ambition in any form—for the group, for individual salvation, or for spiritual achievement—is action postponed. Desire is ever of the future, the desire to become is inaction in the present. The now has greater significance than the tomorrow. In the now is all time, and to understand the now is to be free of time. ...Being is always in the present, and being is the highest form of transformation." (26 : 11).

"What you are now, what you do now, matters tremendously. But those people who believe in a future birth don't give a pin about what happens now. It is just a matter of belief. ...Eternity, that which is timeless, is **now**, not in some distant future. To inquire into that, one must understand the whole problem of time. ...The time that thought has invented as a gradual process of change." (14 : 83).

## 13-8 (128) PASSIVE AWARENESS

Being passively aware means looking, seeing, without bringing in the past, i.e., what is already known. But we usually carry the burden of the past and look, observe, through the screen of the known. This is a form of distraction, and results in partial attention. It prevents total attention. Hence, there is no direct perception and no understanding of any problem. Krishnamurti has explained this and has brought out the importance of passive awareness as follows:

"If I want to understand you, I have to be passively aware; then you begin to tell me all your story. Surely that is not a question of capacity or specialisation." (24 : 69).

"Most of us are incapable of being passively aware, letting the problem tell the story without our interpreting it." (24 : 70).

"What may appear to be small, limited, if approached rightly, reveals the fathomless. It is like a funnel, the narrow opens into the wide. When observed with passive watchfulness, the limited reveals the limitless." (27 : 85).

## 13-9 (154) SELF-ABANDONMENT

## 13-10 (158) SENSITIVENESS

## 13-11 (160) SIMPLICITY

**See all the above categories under 13-1 (4) ANONYMITY.**

# GROUP NO. 14

## 14-1 (7) ATTENTION

Attention means applying the mind fully, without any distraction or diffusion to a subject, which may be a thing, a situation, an idea or thought. It means observing with all energy, with an intention to understand. It involves passive awareness. It is like a powerful beam of light. It reveals **what is**. Attention takes place in a deeply silent state of mind and results in knowing oneself, i.e., self-knowledge. Krishnamurti himself obviously could give total attention, but he could not make it possible for any one of us to do that. It is impossible, because here one has to be a light unto oneself. But it would surely be very relevant and useful to see what he has said about attention. Here are his actual words:

"To be aware of your inattention is of the greatest importance, not how to be attentive all the time. It is greed that asks the question, 'How can I be attentive all the time?' One gets lost in the practice of being attentive. The practice of being attentive is inattention." (25 : 245).

"There cannot be complete attention if there is effort, conflict, resistance, concentration. ...Complete attention is not possible when there is condemnation, justification, or identification, or when the mind is clouded by conclusions, theories." (27 : 51).

"To see the false as the false is attention. The false as the false cannot be seen when there is opinion, judgement, evaluation, attachment, and so on, which are the result of non-attention. Seeing the whole fabric of non-attention is total attention." (10 : 105).

"Out of total attention comes not only energy—which means passion—but also that problem comes to an end. In the same way all images come to an end instantly when there is no preference for an image; this is very important. When you have no preference you have no prejudice. Then you are attentive, then you can look. In that observation there is not only the understanding of the building of images, but also the ending of all images." (14 : 339).

Attention gives rise to awareness, direct experience, and spontaneity, because there is no impediment in the form of choice, condemnation, or justification. There is simplicity, i.e., directness, which makes for immediate, spontaneous action. It is not an action mediated by past knowledge or the known. This is explained by the sage in the following words:

"When thought is in operation there is no silence, there is no awareness. Awareness or perception implies a state of seeing in which there is no image whatsoever." (14 : 469).

The sage has explained direct perception and spontaneous action with the help of an example thus:

"When you see a snake what takes place? ...You run, kill it, do something, why? Because you know it is dangerous. You are aware of the danger of it. A cliff, better take a cliff, an abyss. You know the danger of it. Nobody has to tell you. You see directly what would happen." (14 : 35).

## 14-2 (10) AWARENESS

**See under 14-1 (7) ATTENTION.**

## 14-3 (38) DIRECT EXPERIENCE

**See under 14-1 (7) ATTENTION.**

## 14-4 (96) KNOWING ONESELF

**See under MAHĀVĀKYA No. 2, Chapter 2.**

## 14-5 (156) SELF-KNOWLEDGE

**See under MAHĀVĀKYA No. 2, Chapter 2.**

## 14-6 (164) SPONTANEITY

**See under 14-1 (7) ATTENTION.**

# GROUP NO. 15

## 15-1 (9) AUTHORITY

Authority plays a very influential role in human life. It may be vested in a tradition, a person, a book. The authority is usually never to be questioned and supposed to be followed with devotion, confidence, faith and reverence. A traditionally-minded Hindu would place the highest authority in religious and spiritual matters in the Veda and the Upanishads, but not a Jain or a Buddhist. Every religion has its own authority to be followed strictly by its adherents. Krishnamurti had a peculiarly unfavourable and antagonistic view about any form of authority which he considered as always leading to illusion, strife and conflict. Freedom from authority was his very first demand for understanding and wisdom to come into being. He said:

"The worship of authority, whether in big or little things, is evil, the more so in religious matters. There is no intermediary between you and reality; and if there is one, he is a pretender, a mischief-maker. It does not matter **who** he is, whether the highest saviour or your latest guru or teacher." (26 : 66).

"Be free of all kind of authority, which means, be a light unto yourself. Don't depend on anybody for the understanding of life. ...There must be freedom from the authority of another. ...It means to be able to stand alone." (15 : 8).

"Conformity to the authority of the dead or the living gives intense satisfaction. The teacher knows and you do not know. It would be foolish for you to try to find out anything for yourself when your comforting teacher already knows. So you become his slave, and slavery is better than confusion." (27 : 102-103).

"We do not know ourselves, but we are willing to serve or follow him who promises a reward, a hope, a utopia. Our desires, our cravings are so strong that they drive us into illusions and endless miseries." (26 : 73).

## 15-2 (28) CONFORMITY

**See under 15-1 (9) AUTHORITY.**

## 15-3 (65) FOLLOWING ANOTHER

**See under 15-1 (9) AUTHORITY.**

## 15-4 (100) LIGHT UNTO ONESELF

**See under Mahāvākya No. 10, Chapter 2.**

## 15-5 (125) OTHERS CAN'T HELP

**See under Mahāvākya No. 10, Chapter 2.**

## 15-6 (130) PATHLESS TRUTH

We have discussed what Krishnamurti means by 'truth' under Mahāvākya No. 5 in Chapter 2. He means by truth 'looking at **what is**.' And looking needs no path. It is very important to understand this fact.

Every religion or sect is believed to show a path to truth, and although there may be many different paths they all are supposed to lead to the same truth. Krishnamurti declared in the

Star Congress on 3rd August 1929 at Ommen camp in Holland, "I maintain that truth is a pathless land, and you cannot approach it by any path whatever, by any religion, by any sect."

What did he mean by this statement? Let us see it in his own words.

"Truth has no path, and that is the beauty of truth, it is living. A dead thing has a path to it because it is static. But when you see that truth is something living, moving, ...which is in no temple, mosque or church, which no religion, no teacher, no philosopher, nobody can lead you to — then you will also see that this living thing **is** what you actually are — your anger, your brutality, your violence, your despair, the agony and sorrow you live in. In the understanding of all this is the truth, and you can understand it only if you know how to look at those things in your life." (21 : 15).

"To look needs no philosophy, no teacher. Nobody need tell you how to look, you just look." (21 : 16).

## GROUP NO. 16

### 16-1 (12) BELIEF

To have beliefs is a peculiar quality of the human mind. Some of these beliefs are true; many of them may be false, but we do not know that they are false. Most human beings are gullible and credulous. But a few are not apt to believe readily and easily. They entertain doubts, and these are needed to be cleared before they start believing. Freedom from beliefs is necessary for self-knowledge. Krishnamurti has stressed this point in many of his statements. He has said:

"A belief, religious or political, obviously hinders the understanding of ourselves. It acts as a screen through which we are looking at ourselves. ...If we have no beliefs with which the mind has identified itself, then the mind, without identification, is capable of looking at itself as it is—and then, surely, there is the beginning of the understanding of oneself." (24 : 35).

"If an individual has capacity, then belief becomes a potent thing in his hands, a weapon more dangerous than a gun. For most of us belief has greater meaning than actuality. The understanding of **what is** does not require belief; on the contrary, belief, idea, prejudice is a definite hindrance to understanding. But we prefer our beliefs, our dogmas; they warm us, they promise, they encourage." (26 : 73).

"Belief can never lead to reality. Belief is the result of conditioning, or the outcome of fear, or the result of an outer or inner authority which gives comfort. Reality is none of these. It is something wholly different, and there is no passage from this to that. ...The credulous are always willing to believe, accept, obey, whether what is offered is good or bad, mischievous or beneficial. The believing mind is not an inquiring mind." (25 : 149).

"To find out, one must be free of belief, for belief is the quality of mind that invests in something that will give it some hope, comfort, security, a sense of permanency. To be free to inquire one must be free from fear, from anxiety, from the desire to be psychologically secure. These are the obvious requirements for a very earnest and serious person who wants to find out." (6 : 49).

In this last statement noted above, Krishnamurti has mentioned a very crucial truth about why most of us do not have the capacity to understand truth or reality. It is because we are not free to inquire. We are inflicted by beliefs which deprive us of the freedom that is most essential if one is to be able to find out.

## 16-2 (16) BONDAGE

**See under 16-4 (26) CONDITIONING.**

## 16-3 (25) CONCLUSION

**See under 16-4 (26) CONDITIONING.**

## 16-4 (26) CONDITIONING

'Conditioning' is a word with special importance in Krishnamurti's teachings. Unless one understands its significance very clearly, there would be no understanding of the teachings of the sage.

It means all that we gather from various sources in our life since childhood—the notions, ideas, concepts, beliefs, emotional reaction patterns, knowledge, opinions, conclusions, and so on. Most of it is accepted by us without judging it critically or evaluating it with an open mind. Another word often used by Krishnamurti for conditioning is 'the past'. One very peculiar fact about it is that we are not aware of its existence and the tremendous role it plays in our life. So long as we are unaware of it, conflict and misery keep on playing havoc in our life. And we go on endlessly gathering more and more of it, thinking that thereby we may find a way out of our suffering. Krishnamurti has described the nature of conditioning, its cause, and removal in the following passages.

"In the Christian myth of original sin and in the whole eastern doctrine of **samsāra** one sees that the factor of conditioning has been felt, though rather obscurely. If it had been clearly seen, naturally these doctrines and myths would not have arisen. ...This struggle to become is time in which there is confusion and the greed for the more and better. The 'me' seeks security and not finding it transfers the search to heaven. The very 'me' that identifies itself with something greater in which it hopes to lose itself—whether that be the nation, the ideal or some god—is the factor of conditioning." (25 : 278-279).

"We are the result of the thoughts and influences of others; we are conditioned by religious as well as political propaganda. ...Organised religions are first-rate propagandists, every means being used to pursuade and then to hold." (26 : 62).

"When the mind realises the totality of its own conditioning—which it cannot do as long as it is merely pursuing its own comfort, or lazily taking the easy course—then all its movements come to an end; it is completely still, without any desire, without any compulsion, without any motive. Only then is there freedom." (28 : 60).

"We are so heavily conditioned that we never look, never ask, never question, never doubt. We are all followers, we are all yes-sayers. ...If you are clear, you will never follow anybody.

And when you follow somebody, out of your confusion, you will create more confusion. So what you have to do is to stop first, enquire, look, listen." (20 : 59).

## 16-5 (45) DOGMA

Dogma means the spiritual and religious beliefs to which we hold very steadfastly. **See under 16-1 (12) BELIEF.**

## 16-6 (47) DREAMS

Dreams are looked upon by psychologists as a phenomenon very essential for release of tension. Most of us are full of tension in daily life and many of our desires remain unfulfilled or partially fulfilled. They give rise to constant tension in the mind. In dreams we see some of our desires fulfilled, and that helps to discharge tensions. Dreams thus serve a useful purpose like a safety valve. But Krishnamurti's own experience seems to be different. He has emphasised the role of the absence of dreams. One who does not have tensions of any kind during waking life would not be having any dreams in sleep. This he has pointed out clearly. But most common people do have dreams as a necessary and unavoidable phenomenon of daily life. He has said:

"It is very important to have a mind that is completely quiet when you are asleep. Then the whole mind, the whole brain, the whole body can rejuvenate itself. But if the brain goes on working while you are asleep, then it becomes exhausted, therefore neurotic, overstrained and all the rest of it. So is it possible not to dream at all?" (14 : 322).

"Can the mind be completely still during sleep? This is possible, but only when the travail of the day is understood at each minute so that it is finished and not carried over. ...Then the mind is completely at rest." (14 : 156-157).

## 16-7 (74) HABIT

Habit in the various types of manual work means a reflex action, a development of skill which results in effortless, smooth, easygoing work. It makes daily life skilful and easy. But habit in the intellectual, psychological field creates very difficult problems. There, habit means lack of alertness and absence of sensitiveness, questioning, doubting. It leads to blind following. Krishnamurti has emphasised this point as follows:

"Why does the mind fall into habit? It is the easiest way to live; it is easy to live mechanically. Sexually and in every other way it is easy to live that way. I can live life without effort, change, because in that I find complete security. In habit there is no examination, searching, asking. ...Habit implies conclusions, formulas, ideas, principles. All these are habits. Habit is the essence of the observer." (19 : 132-133).

## 16-8 (84) IGNORANCE

To ignore means not to pay due attention. In politics, the wrongdoings of party leaders are ignored by party members. Ignorance means not having correct knowledge. This is of two types: (*i*) absence or lack of knowledge, and (*ii*) having illusory notions or falsities as knowledge, i.e., having false beliefs. Krishnamurti does not give much importance to ignorance in this sense. His main interest is in ignorance of a special kind, and he has used the term **ignorance** in his own peculiar, restricted sense. He means by ignorance, "not knowing the real nature of the 'me' or self", i.e., 'not having self-knowledge'. He has stressed this point in several statements, some of which are given below:

"Ignorance is the lack of self-awareness; and knowledge is ignorance when there is no understanding of the ways of the self." (26 : 26).

"Without self-knowledge there can be no right thinking, and then all knowledge is ignorance, which can only lead to confusion and destruction." (26 : 47).

"Suffering exists so long as there is ignorance of the whole process of one's own being. So long as I do not know myself, the ways and compulsions of my mind, unconscious as well as conscious, there must be suffering. After all we suffer because of ignorance—ignorance in the sense of not knowing ourself. ...Without self-knowledge suffering will continue." (18 : 10).

"Surely, by understanding what is false, what is illusion, what is ignorance, truth comes into being." (18 : 11).

"You must know yourself. Immaturity lies only in total ignorance of self. To understand yourself is the beginning of wisdom." (21 : 12).

## 16-9 (85) ILLUSION

Illusions, misconceptions, wrong notions, wild imaginations form a very common feature of the daily life of man all over the world. Illusions are liked by us because they are more attractive as compared to what may be true, the actual. Our forefathers entertained many illusions like the existence of ghosts, angels, damsels, witches, and so on. Boons and curses were formerly taken to come true. Many religious beliefs such as the dead coming to life, gods and goddesses appearing before devotees in superhuman forms, and the like, were nothing more than misbeliefs. But their influence on the human mind was very strong, simply tremendous, in the past. With the progress of science some of these illusions have now been given up completely. Krishnamurti tried hard throughout his life to make us aware of the importance of being free from the influence of illusions, although in his earlier life he had co-operated readily to propagate and promote the illusions of Theosophy taught to him by Leadbeater and Annie Besant. His views are mentioned below:

"**What should be** is the idea, the fiction and so there is conflict between the actual and the illusion. ...We like the illusion better than the actual; the idea is more appealing, more satisfying, and so we cling to it. Thus the illusion becomes the real and the actual becomes the false." (26 : 86).

Illusion has an important place in our life so long as our life is guided by becoming, the desire to be something or to have something. With most of us, this desire is an unending, unmistakable, unavoidable characteristic of life. This fact is brought out by the sage in very few words in the following statement:

"The craving for experience is the beginning of illusion." (28 : 7).

## 16-10 (122) OPINION

Opinion indicates lack of complete knowledge. In our life many a time there arise occasions when complete and definite information about something is not possible to gain. Under such a situation opinion, i.e., one among a few possible views, is required to be accepted and action to be taken according to that opinion. Opinions of experts, scientists, often differ, but they are ready to give up an opinion held by them and accept a new point of view on the basis of further information. Krishnamurti has discussed 'opinion' in the spiritual and religious fields. That is somewhat different from the Opinion mentioned above. It is found to prevent knowing 'what is'. He has said:

"Opinion, and the exploration of opinion, is not truth. ...Opinion is always biased, coloured by the culture, the education, the knowledge one has. Why should the mind be burdened with opinions at all, with what you think about this or that person, or book, or idea? Why shouldn't the mind be empty? Only when it is empty can it see clearly. ...It is opinion and belief that prevent the observation of what actually is." (25 : 118-119).

## 16-11 (136) PRISON

Prison is where one has no freedom. One is restricted in action. In a way all of us are prisoners. We live in the prison of our desires, cravings, beliefs, likes and dislikes, the idea that '**I am this**' and '**I want to be that**'. To be free from this prison means to understand '**what is**' from moment to moment. This is a very important, very basic truth of the teachings of J. Krishnamurti. We are never usually aware of this truth and we pass our whole life in a prison of our own making. The sage has explained this truth in the following statements:

"One can be inwardly simple, surely, only by understanding the innumerable impediments, attachments, fears, in which one is held. But most of us **like** to be held—by people, by possessions, by ideas. We like to be prisoners. Inwardly we **are** prisoners. ...of our desires, of our wants, of our ideals, of innumerable motivations. ...As we proceed to investigate the inward complexities of our being, we become more and more sensitive, free." (24 : 63-64).

"When a mind is programmed, it says, I am a Hindu, or Muslim and so on, I am this, I am that, ...It is not free, because it is merely repeating. Be clear on this point. Only a mind that is free from all programmes is a free mind. Because we are prisoners we want to be free. But that opposite is not freedom." (8 : 2).

## 16-12 (155) SELF-DECEPTION

Words like illusion, self-hypnosis and self-deception are used in the teachings of J. Krishnamurti as synonyms. When we project an idea from the duality of 'I am this' and 'I want to be that', that projection can never lead to truth because it is based on escaping from **what is**, and not facing it. But a very peculiar feature of such a projection, such a running away, is that we are never aware of the falsity of it. We never understand it as false, as an illusion, as a self-deception. We are just led adrift by our craving, and this fact is something which we are never aware of. Krishnamurti makes us aware of this fundamental nature of self-deception in the following statement:

"Self-deception exists when there is any form of craving or attachment: attachment to a prejudice, to an experience, to a system of thought. Consciously or unconsciously the experiencer is always seeking greater, deeper, wider experience; and as long as the experiencer exists, there must be delusion in one form or another." (28 : 8).

## 16-13 (181) VISIONS

Many of us have visions of meeting god, our guru, or some other person. We even get hints about future happenings. It is believed that apart from the gross body we have an astral body and a few of us are supposed to be able to move in the astral body and communicate with persons who are far away just like we meet persons in this, our natural body made of bones and muscles. Krishnamurti was himself a party to this obviously false belief at the behest of Charles Webster Leadbeater, his mentor, in his childhood and early youth. But in his later life, after being free from self-deception, he had this to say about the visions:

"You can have marvellous experiences and yet be completely deluded. You will inevitably see visions according to your conditioning: you will see Christ or Buddha or whoever you happen to believe in, and the greater a believer you are the stronger will be your visions, the projections of your own demands and urges." (21 : 112).

"The vision is the projection of the particular tradition which happens to form the background of the mind. This conditioning, not the vision which it projects, is the actuality, the fact. To understand the fact is simple; but it is made difficult by our likes and dislikes, by our condemnation of the fact, by the opinions or judgements we have about the fact. To be free of these various forms of evaluation is to understand the actual, the **what is**." (28 : 146).

## GROUP NO. 17

### 17-1 (46) DOUBT

Doubt is usually considered a sin in religion and the spiritual field. On the other hand, devotion, attachment, identification, and credulousness (**shraddhā**) are considered to be great virtues which are admired and praised by gurus, saints, mahants and yogis, and those followers who have these qualities are encouraged by them. However, these tendencies are to be shunned because they prevent understanding and being aware of **what is**. Krishnamurti has described the great value of doubt in inquiry into truth, intelligence, reality and wisdom. Here are his own words:

"Doubt is a precious thing. It cleanses, purifies the mind. ...The whole concept of regeneration and the Christian belief and dogma of resurrection, ...also the Asiatic world's acceptance that there is continuity—in doubting, questioning all that, there is a certain freedom which is necessary for our inquiry. If you can put all that aside, actually, not merely verbally but negate all that deep within oneself, then one has no illusion. And it is necessary to be totally free from any kind of illusion—the illusions that are imposed upon us and the illusions that we create for ourselves ...there must be freedom of opinion and judgement." (11 : 25).

## 17-2 (49) EDUCATION

Giving proper education to boys and girls in schools—that was perhaps the only activity or programe undertaken by Krishnamurti, apart from giving talks and discourses. Otherwise, for understanding **what is**, he never advocated any effort or discipline (**sādhanā**). His talks were naturally stopped after his death (although there are audio and video cassettes in which those talks are preserved). But the schools continued working. He had started them with a view to provide a congenial atmosphere for inner change to take place in the minds of students. But actually, just as no one from his audiences was transformed or underwent any inner revolution, regeneration or mutation by hearing his talks, similarly, through the schools, to repeat his own words, "no one, no student, flowered". But still, his views on education were very remarkable and enlightening for all of us. We must try to understand them adequately, in their proper context. He said:

"The function of education is to give the student abundant knowledge in the various fields of human endeavour and at the same time to free his mind from all tradition so that he is able to investigate, to find out, to discover. Otherwise the mind becomes mechanical, burdened with the machinery of knowledge." (24 : 147).

"Education is not only learning from books, memorising some facts, but also learning how to look, how to listen to what the books are saying, whether they are saying something true or false. ...It is also to be able to listen to the birds, to see the sky, to see the extraordinary beauty of a tree, and the shape of the hills." (9 : 11).

"To understand life is much more important than merely to prepare for examinations and become very proficient in maths, physics, or what you will." (24 : 93).

## 17-3 (91) INTEGRALLY INTELLIGENT

To be an expert, to be learned, means to be proficient, to have excellence in a branch of knowledge or technique. We have many such persons in any society, and they command respect for their expertise. But they may not be happy in their life due to that knowledge or skill. Life may not be free of tension and misery for them at all. We actually find many of these learned professors or professionals to be very unhappy, ill-adjusted with their surroundings. For happiness, bliss, tension-free life, being learned, skilful in a branch of knowledge or profession is not enough, adequate. It does not necessarily make for happiness. For that, one needs to be 'integrally intelligent'. This is a phrase coined by Krishnamurti, which all of us should know well, in order to understand clearly the state of wisdom which is not one-sided but all-inclusive. He has said:

"Most of us are intelligent in layers, you probably in one way and I in some other way. Some of you are intelligent in your business work, some others in your laboratory work, and so on; people are intelligent in different ways; but we are not integrally intelligent. To be integrally intelligent means to be without the self." (24 : 54).

## 17-4 (99) LEARNING

In life we are required to learn many things from others. It is a process which goes on from childhood, through adulthood up to old age. Krishnamurti has given great importance to learning in his teaching. According to him learning is not mere acquisition of information, facts and skills. It means the art of thinking clearly, having no illusions and false beliefs, and being free from fictitious goals and ideals. This is a rather peculiar but very important view. He has said:

"By learning I do not mean the mere cultivation of memory or the accumulation of knowledge but the capacity to think clearly and sanely without illusion, to start from facts and not from beliefs and ideals." (12 : 8).

"When you are really learning you are learning throughout your life. ...Then everything teaches you ...a dead leaf, a bird in flight, a smell, a tear, the rich and the poor, the smile of a woman, the haughtiness of a man. You learn from everything." (24 : 222).

"Once you begin to learn, there is no end to learning." (9 : 17).

## 17-5 (101) LISTENING

When we listen to something, or even when we read something, two processes go on simultaneously in our mind. One is grasping the meaning of what is being heard or read, and the other is of judging, comparing, examining, accepting or rejecting it on the basis of what we already know, believe, like or dislike. Thus we understand not directly, impartially, with total attention, but through the screen of our conditioning, our prejudices, our past. This fact is emphasised by Krishnamurti in the following statements:

"Surely, one listens only when the mind is not translating what it hears, in terms of what it knows. Knowledge prevents listening. ...How can one see whether a statement is true or false, if one's mind is prejudiced, caught in the framework of its own or another's conclusions and experiences? For such a mind what is important is to be aware of its own limitations." (28 : 97-98).

"When you observe your conditioning, the conditioning exists only in the observer, not in the observed. When you look without the observer, without the 'me', his fears, his anxieties, and all the rest of it, then you will see, you enter into a totally different dimension." (14 : 89).

"If you are listening with total abandonment, you have done everything you can possibly do, because then you are seeing the truth as it is the truth of every day, of every action, of every thought, of every field." (20 : 72).

## 17-6 (103) LOOKING

As for listening, so for looking. Our act of looking is never direct. It is always accompanied by distractions caused by our thoughts, memories, and what is known. In the following passages Krishnamurti has made this point clear:

"Apparently it is one of the most difficult things for a human being to look at anything directly, not through images, opinions, conclusions, which are all symbols." (25 : 267).

"Most of us condemn, or explain away or justify—we never look without justification or condemnation. Therefore the first thing to do—and probably it is the last thing to do—is to observe without any form of condemnation. This is going to be very difficult because all our culture, our tradition, is to compare, justify or condemn what we are ...which prevents us from actually observing what we are." (6 : 16).

"If we know how to look then the whole thing becomes very clear, and to look needs no philosophy, no teacher. Nobody need tell you how to look. You just look." (21 : 16).

"Seeing is of the greatest importance. Seeing is attention, and it is only inattention that gives rise to a problem." (25 : 244).

## 17-7 (151) SEEING

**See under 17-6 (103) LOOKING.**

## 17-8 (170) TOTAL ACTION

**See under 14-1 (7) ATTENTION.**

## 17-9 (171) TOTAL ATTENTION

**See under 14-1 (7) ATTENTION.**

# GROUP NO. 18

## 18-1 (2) AMBITION

Krishnamurti looks upon ambition as a cause of disharmony and misery in human life. It breeds conflict at various levels and results in cruelty and treachery. For a congenial human relationship, ambition must be totally overcome. He has explained this in the following statements:

"If we would live at peace with each other, surely, ambition must completely come to an end—not only political, economic, social ambition, but also the more subtle and pernicious ambition, the spiritual ambition—to **be** something." (24 : 39).

"Life is more intimate among the less educated, where the fever of ambition has not yet spread. The boy smiles at you, the old woman wonders, the man hesitates and passes by." (26 : 242).

"Ambition, whether personal or identified with the collective, is always antisocial. So-called noble ambition in a relationship is fundamentally destructive." (12 : 8).

## 18-2 (3) ANGER

Anger is a state of mind which Krishnamurti has discussed on several occasions. We do not like to be angry. But on the spur of the moment it is never possible not to be angry. A second or two later when we think about it, we dislike anger. The sage has said that anger can be got rid of by understanding and thereby overcoming desire. His words are mentioned below:

"Most of us do not mind being angry. ...We never just say we are angry, and stop there. We go into elaborate explanations of its cause. ...Violently or softly we blame someone else. ...Anger cannot be got rid of by the action of will, for will is part of violence. Will is the outcome of desire, the craving to be; and desire in its very nature is aggressive, dominant. ...To be free from violence ...there must be the understanding of desire." (26 : 70-71).

## 18-3 (22) CHATTERING MIND

The unsteadiness of the mind, its lack of stability, stillness and silence, is a quality experienced by every one of us. Krishnamurti has discussed the chattering nature of the human mind and its consequences. He has said that learning and understanding is possible only when there is attention and no chattering. Attention can be possible only when the mind is silent and not distracted. Distraction is overcome only when desire is understood directly, immediately. All these points are brought out by the sage in the following statements:

"It is important to have a mind that is not constantly occupied, constantly chattering. To an unoccupied mind a new seed of learning can germinate—something entirely different from the cultivation of knowledge and acting from that knowledge." (17 : 202).

"You can only listen when there is no self-projected noise. When you are chattering to yourself, comparing what is being said with what you already know, then you are not listening. When you are observing with your eyes and all kinds of prejudices and knowledge are interfering, you are not really observing." (6 : 54-55).

"If you are chattering, if your mind is constantly in movement, rushing all over the place, obviously it cannot look, it cannot listen totally." (14 : 97).

## 18-4 (23) COMPARISON

Comparison is a psychological process which every human being adopts, learns, since childhood. We are always comparing ourselves with others insofar as various qualities and characteristics are concerned. We always behave with others on the basis of the comparison between us. It is not a conscious process. It goes on unknowingly, without our being aware of it. Krishnamurti has pointed out a fact of great importance, namely, that this habit of comparing is at the root of conflict, disharmony, disorder and suffering. Here are his own statements:

"We, from childhood, are trained to compare. ...Comparing, measuring and all this breeds compromise, which is a tremendous wastage of energy." (14 : 202).

"Measuring ourselves all the time against something or someone is one of the primary causes of conflict. ...This comparison has been taught from childhood. ...When you do not compare at all, when there is no ideal, no opposite, no factor of duality, when you no longer struggle to be different from what you are ...your mind has ceased to create the opposite, and has become highly intelligent, highly sensitive, capable of immense passion." (21 : 64).

"Most people think that learning is encouraged through comparison, whereas the contrary is the fact. Comparison brings about frustration and merely encourages envy, which is called competition." (12 : 8).

## 18-5 (24) CONCENTRATION

**See under 8-1 (107) MEDITATION.**

## 18-6 (27) CONFLICT

Conflict is a situation arising out of clashing or diverse interests in a relationship. When interests do not clash, when they are congenial, co-operative, not against each other, there may be no occasion for conflict. But conflict is actually a hard reality of life for each and every human being. Even if a person realises the state of transformation, freedom, understanding and wisdom, conflict may be imposed on such a person by others in a relationship, and he may not necessarily be free from conflict. One cannot always stop others from creating conflict. But one may, indeed, be free from being afflicted by conflict perpetrated by others. Krishnamurti's discussion of conflict refers to this state of inner freedom from conflict and not to the non-existence of conflict. The ending of conflict means the ending of affliction by conflict. Here are some statements of the sage about conflict:

"To end conflict is one of the most complex things. It needs self-observation and the sensitivity of awareness of the outer as well as of the inner. Conflict can only end where there is the understanding of the contradiction in oneself." (25 : 203).

"Conflict is the denial of **what is** or the running away from **what is**; there is no conflict other than that. Our conflict becomes more and more complex and insoluble because we do not face **what is**." (26 : 217).

"When there is a division between human beings—nationalities, religions, social divisions—there must be conflict." (13 : 6).

## 18-7 (31) CONTRADICTION

Contradiction means resistance, division, disorder, disharmony. This becomes a dominant part of life when the 'me' or self acts strongly, when a person has excessive self-concern. Krishnamurti has pointed this out while discussing the role of the centre, the self.

"As long as you are working with a centre... there must be contradiction. That is, as long as you are acting self-centredly, selfishly, egoistically, personally, narrowing the whole of this vast life into that little 'me', you will inevitably create disorder. The 'me' is a very small affair put together by thought. So long as there is self-centred activity there must be contradiction, there must be disorder." (15 : 6).

## 18-8 (42) DISORDER

Disorder means lack of understanding, lack of freedom, lack of wisdom. Human life is so full of disorder, so devoid of order that disorder may be pointed out as one of the most outstanding marks of human affairs, human relationships. Krishnamurti has pointed out the very vital role of understanding disorder for the establishment of order. Order is not to be pursued positively. It means the negation of disorder. This is a subtle and most significant truth brought out by him. The following statements make this point clear:

"The primary cause of disorder in ourselves is the seeking of reality promised by another. We mechanically follow some body who will assure us a comfortable spiritual life. ...If we reject all so-called spiritual authority, all ceremonies, rituals and dogmas, it means that we stand alone and are already in a conflict with society; we cease to be respectable human beings." (21 : 11).

"When you understand the structure of disorder, that very understanding brings about discipline, discipline not of suppression, not of imitation. Out of negation comes the right discipline, which is order." (20 : 79).

"When you understand the nature of disorder, out of that comprehension, out of the depth of understanding of the nature of disorder comes, naturally, order. Order is like a flower coming out naturally, and that order, that flower, never withers." (15 : 5-6).

## 18-9 (43) DISTRACTION

'Attention' and 'distraction' are two very important words in the vocabulary of J. Krishnamurti. Attention means listening, observing, attending to anything, a person, or an event or idea or thing with full engrossment, without moving away. But we hardly ever do this, because our minds are unsteady. They are full of cravings, beliefs, and conclusions, which keep on pulling them in various directions. That causes distraction. The following statement of the sage explains it:

"Our own thoughts and judgements are so much more important to us than to find out **what is**. The **what is** is always simple, it is we who are complex. We make the simple **what is** complex and we get lost in it. We listen only to the increasing noise of our own confusion. To listen we must be free. It is not that there must be no distractions, for thinking itself is a form of distraction." (26 : 246).

The last sentence of the above statement is of the utmost importance. It says a very crucial fact about thought, which we should never overlook or forget.

## 18-10 (58) ESCAPES

Escape is one of the most important key words of the teachings of J. Krishnamurti. It indicates a very significant fact about the human mind, namely, that in the face of suffering, sorrow, which every one of us meets in life again and again, our habitual reaction is to run away, instead of meeting it squarely. Thinking, condemning, imitation, following others, identification are various forms of escape which we take recourse to, for avoiding suffering. Krishnamurti has shown below how escape is an inadequate, unintelligent reaction. He has also pointed out what the adequate, intelligent thing is that one should do.

"Our attachment to a person, to work, to an ideology, is the conditioning factor. This is the thing we have to understand and not seek a better or more intelligent escape. All escapes are unintelligent, as they inevitably bring about conflict. To cultivate detachment is another form of escape, of isolation. ...The ideal is an escape from **what is**. There is the understanding of **what is**, an adequate action towards **what is**, only when the mind is no longer seeking any escape. The very thinking about **what is** is an escape from **what is**. Thinking about the problem is an escape from the problem; for thinking **is** the problem and the only problem. The mind, unwilling to be what it is, fearful of what it is, seeks these various escapes; and the way of escape is thought. As long as there is thinking, there must be escapes, attachments, which only strengthen conditioning." (27 : 5-6).

"It appears that man has always escaped from himself, from what he is, from where he is going... It is strange that we never realise that however much we may escape from ourselves... the conflict, the pleasure, the pain, the fear and so on are always there. ...You can't escape from this deep, unfathomed turmoil unless you really give thought to it, not only thought but see by careful attention, diligent watching, the whole movement of thought and the self." (11 : 48-49).

## 18-11 (121) OCCUPIED MIND

It is a peculiarity of the human mind that it is never silent, still, but always occupied and unsteady. How to stop the mind from being occupied so that it can know the state of being silent and still is a very difficult problem with which many of us have battled. Krishnamurti has discussed this problem in various ways. Here are two of his statements on the occupied mind:

"You cannot study the problem fully if your mind is occupied too eagerly with finding an answer." (24 : 239).

"It is important to have a mind that is not constantly occupied, constantly chattering." (17 : 202).

## 18-12 (123) OPPOSITES

In the teachings of J. Krishnamurti some words have come to assume a special significance which they do not enjoy in common parlance. 'Opposite' is one such word. Krishnamurti has coined phrases like 'the conflict of opposites', 'the wheel of opposites', which are particularly important in understanding Krishnamurti's teachings. Man's life on earth has been such that out of the many desires and cravings arising in the human mind only a few are fulfilled and many remain unfulfilled for a long time or forever. This gives rise to duality in the mind like '**I am this**' and '**I**

**want to be that**', or in other words, the duality between '**what is**' and '**what should be**'. In this duality, the '**that**' is nothing but a projection of the mind. It has no reality. It is just a prejudice, an idea, an imagination of the mind out of its disappointment due to the thwarting of a desire. That projection or idea is the opposite which is posited, imagined, as an ideal to be achieved in future. Krishnamurti has explained this process as follows:

"Change implies a movement from **what is** to something different. ...All opposites are mutually dependent, like hot and cold, high and low. ...The opposite exists only in comparison. So change to an opposite is no change at all. ...It is an illusion." (25 : 187).

"When the mind becomes aware of being in a constant state of flux, it proceeds to build the opposite of that state, thereby getting caught in the conflict of duality; and then, wanting to escape from this conflict, it pursues still another opposite. So the mind is bound to the wheel of opposites." (28 : 18).

## 18-13 (152) SEEKING

Human life is very largely a matter of seeking, failing and achieving. In everyday life, seeking is most essential. But many of us are seekers of religious and spiritual goals, and there seeking is an illusory affair because the goal is usually a projection of the mind based on its conditioning. Krishnamurti was very emphatic on this point. He said:

"Not to seek any form of experience is very difficult; most of our lives are so mechanical, so shallow, that we want deeper experiences because we are bored with the superficiality of life. We want, or rather crave for something that will have a meaning, a fullness, depth, beauty, loveliness, and so the mind is seeking. And what it seeks, it will find; what it finds will not be the truth." (6 : 124).

Why shall it not be the truth? This is an important question. The obvious answer to this question is that what we seek in the religious and spiritual fields is born of an illusion, a projection of the mind, which arises out of what is believed, known, accepted from others. It is just an imagination which is very different from **what is**. So Krishnamurti has said:

"That is the first thing to learn—not to seek. When you seek you are really only window-shopping." (21 : 12).

## 18-14 (183) WHAT SHOULD BE

When **what is** is understood, the **what should be** does not arise, and seeking stops. But this does not actually happen in our life because of our habit of escaping, running away, from **what is**, just out of a very strong habit. Krishnamurti has explained this point in the following two statements:

"The understanding of the actual is possible only when the ideal, the **what should be** is erased from the mind; that is, only when the false is seen as the false. The **what should be** is also the **what should not be**." (27 : 84).

"If you understand **what is**, what need is there for **what should be**?" (25 : 183).

# GROUP NO. 19

## 19-1 (32) CORNER OF THE FIELD

The 'corner of the field' is an important phrase coined by the sage. Our understanding should actually engulf the whole field of life, including all its aspects, all the experiences that go to make the whole field of life. But we are usually experts of only a part, a selected field of the whole. With self-knowledge comes the full grasp of the whole of life. Otherwise we specialise in only a corner of the field and remain blank in other fields. This is usually the case with experts and great thinkers who do not possess self-knowledge or wisdom, as the sage understands it. Here are his own words about the matter:

"When you neglect the whole field of life and concentrate only on a little part... you are living unskilfully and therefore you are not an artist of life... This is the greatest art: living skilfully in the whole field of life... there is no way to nourish it, there is no practising of it, there is only the seeing of it." (25 : 256).

"Please do realise this. ...All that one has to do is to see. See the corner, the little house that one has built in a corner of a vast, an immeasurable field; and living there, fighting, quarrelling, see it. And that is why it is very important to understand what it means to see." (14 : 191-192).

"The most fundamental problem for the human being is the question of freedom from 'the little corner'. And that little corner is ourselves... our shoddy little mind." (14 : 194-195).

## 19-2 (44) DIVISION

Division between human beings due to religion, tradition, culture, etc., and the clashes arising from it, have been a topic which the sage has discussed on several occasions. He has mentioned in the following statements how the division could be overcome through a negative approach, instead of pursuing the positive way.

"Organised religion is the cause of division, just like nationality and power groups... The family, the church and the state bring about such division. ...Thought itself is always divisive, so all action based on an idea or ideology is division. Thought cultivates prejudice, opinion, judgement." (25 : 236).

"Through negation we may come upon the positive, but merely to pursue the positive leads to assumptions and conclusions which bring about division." (25 : 237).

## 19-3 (66) FRAGMENTATION

Fragmentation is one of those words which have come to assume great importance in the teachings of J. Krishnamurti, although in common parlance they are not much used at all. Fragment means a part, a limited, divided piece from a whole, separated for any purpose. Fragmentation means a breaking away of a whole into small bits, usually with disharmony among them. Krishnamurti has looked upon it as a cause of misery in human life. He always stressed the need to overcome fragmentation. He said:

"We have divided the world into communist, socialist, imperialist and Catholic, Protestant, Hindu, Buddhist, and nationalities, linguistic divisions; the whole thing is fragmentation. Why has the mind fragmented the whole of life?" (14 : 31).

"Is it possible to look without the observer looking at the thing called the observed? If there is the observer looking, then he must look through fragmentation, through division and where there is division both in myself and outwardly, there must be conflict." (14 : 319).

"We live in fragments. You are one thing at the office, another at home; you talk about democracy and in your heart you are autocratic. ...The only way to look at yourself is totally, immediately, without time; and you can see the totality of yourself only when the mind is not fragmented." (21 : 30).

## 19-4 (90) ISOLATION

**See under 19-2 (44) DIVISION.**

# GROUP NO. 20

## 20-1 (73) GURU

The guru, who is an expert, a guide, is a must when one wants to learn some technique, have some information, or be proficient in some art or science. Such gurus are found to impart training which is essential for one to become fit to earn one's livelihood. But gurus in other fields, that of religious and spiritual training and guidance, are not so useful, so clearly and unquestionably beneficial and justifiable. That is because the goals which they are supposed to lead up to are largely illusory, and associated with make-believe. Krishnamurti has clearly pointed out that the importance given to a guru, master, monk, saint, sannyasi, saviour, is completely out of proportion, totally misplaced, and wholly unwarranted, uncalled for. Here are his actual words:

"The pursuit, all the world over, of gurus and their systems, reading the latest books on this and that, and so on, seems to me so utterly empty, so utterly futile, for you may wander all over the earth, but you have to come back to yourself." (24 : 13).

"Instead of lifting your burden they impose their burden on you. ...The moment the guru says he knows, then you may be sure he doesn't know." (14 : 24).

"Belief in the master creates the master, and experience is shaped by belief. ...One of the easiest escapes is the guru, the master, or a disciple. ...After all, that is what most of us want: to be safe, to be secure. ...The craving for individual or group security brings on destruction, and to be safe psychologically engenders illusion." (26 : 73-74).

"Under the robe the monk is frightened. He has his own appetites, he is burning with desire and the robe is merely an escape from this fact." (25 : 71).

"The chastity of the monk, with his vows and denials, is essentially worldliness, which is unchaste." (7 : 11).

"Money is more important than anything else except power. These two things are a marvellous combination; the saint has power, though he has no money; he is influencing the rich and poor. The politician will use the country, the saint, the gods that be, to come to the top and tell you the absurdity of ambition and the ruthlessness of power." (10 : 213-214).

"Generally the saints are distorted human beings. Because they lead the so-called simple life, the others are greatly impressed; but their minds are twisted, and they create what they think is reality." (20 : 76).

"The sannyāsi has merely renounced the outer show of the world, of society, but inwardly he is still a part of it; he is still burning with the desire to achieve, to gain, to become." (28 : 82).

"When you read or listen to some saint endlessly, or some sannyasi, making commentaries on the Gita or the Upanishads—just think of it! The childishness of it. ...All this shows that immaturity is essentially a waste of energy." (14 : 202).

"There have been so many saviours, masters, gurus, political leaders and philosophers, and not one of them has saved you from your own misery and conflict. So why follow them? Perhaps there may be quite another approach to all our problems." (25 : 37).

## 20-2 (105) MASTER

## 20-3 (111) MONK

## 20-4 (146) SAINT

## 20-5 (147) SANNYASI

## 20-6 (148) SAVIOUR

**See all the above categories under 20-1 (73) GURU.**

# GROUP NO. 21

## 21-1 (5) ATMAN

**Ātman** and **Brahman** are two most prestigious words of Indian philosophy. They represent the basic reality, the ultimate truth, the absolute, transcendental, permanent entity underlying the world, which is transient, and full of decay and death. Krishnamurti did not share this view. We must try to understand his statements carefully and clearly.

"Look, how deceptive the mind has become, caught in words. I have accumulated knowledge about suffering and suffering does not end, and not knowing how to end it, thought says there must be some other factor. So it invents the **ātman**. It thinks about it. Otherwise the **ātman** would not have come into existence. ...The **ātman** does not end suffering either. ...It has no value at all. It is like a man who is hungry and you describe food to him. ...They have destroyed the mind by introducing a factor which does not help." (19 : 185-186).

"To free the mind from all authority there must be self-knowing, that is, self-knowledge. I do not mean the higher self or the **ātman**, which are all the inventions of the mind, the inventions of thought, inventions born out of fear." (20 : 78).

## 21-2 (21) CERTAINTY

**See under 27-2 (78) HUMAN MIND.**

## 21-3 (70) GOD

Man has entertained the idea of God in the form of a conviction, an axiom, a very strongly and fondly held belief for many thousand years. But those who do not take God's existence for granted have also been there since the beginning of the idea of God, although they always formed a very small proportion of the human population at any time. Why does man like it so much to entertain this belief as a self-evident truth? And how did the idea of God arise? These two questions have been considered by Krishnamurti in his talks and writings. We would do well to understand them sincerely and deeply, not merely superficially and casually.

"This is childish and immature thinking. You think the Great Father is watching every one of us. That is a mere projection of your own personal liking. It is obviously not true. Truth must be something entirely different." (24 : 38).

"We demand permanency and create a culture based on this demand, inventing gods, which are not gods at all but merely a projection of our own desires." (24 : 144).

"Man has always sought something beyond knowledge, beyond the response of thought; so he has created an image called God." (6 : 146-147).

"Surely, without the understanding of oneself the search for so-called reality is an escape from oneself. Without self-knowledge the God that you seek is the God of illusion, and illusion inevitably brings conflict and sorrow." (26 : 47).

"The temple, the **pūjā**, the sacred thread—these things are not of God. They are the creations of man's vanity and fear. It is only the unhappy, the frightened who worship God." (29 : 132).

## 21-4 (87) IMPERMANENCE

**See under Mahāvākya 11, Chapter 2.**

## 21-5 (132) PERMANENCE

**See under Mahāvākya 11, Chapter 2.**

## 21-6 (150) SECURITY

Security regarding food, shelter and clothing, the primary needs of life, is most essential for every one of us. In developing countries like India a large population lives below the poverty line, and their primary needs are not properly met. Krishnamurti has discussed the problem of security in case of those whose primary needs are fulfilled, yet, they suffer from the desire to be psychologically secure, seeking a permanent reality. That goal is an illusion. He has explained their problem as follows:

"We want to be secure inwardly and also spiritually by erecting walls of belief which are an indication of the craving to be certain." (24 : 37).

"Most of us are seeking to build walls around ourselves so as to be invulnerable, but unfortunately there is always an opening through which life creeps in. ...Most people, including the so-called religious, desire abiding peace, a state in which all conflict has come to an end." (27 : 88).

"To find out for yourself that there is no form of security in any relationship, to realise that psychologically there is nothing permanent, gives a totally different approach to life... one can discipline the mind, control it, shape it. But such torture does not make the mind quiet. It merely makes it dull." (21 : 107).

## 21-7 (176) UNCERTAINTY

Security and certainty always go together in our mind. We desire to have both. But they are always elusive. There is nothing permanent, nothing secure. Of course, we do experience them in life sporadically, on some occasions, for some time. But there is always a possibility of disturbance caused by this or that reason. The following statement of the sage describes this clearly.

"Can the mind be free from the desire for security? That is the problem, not what to believe and how much to believe. These are merely expressions of the inward craving to be secure psychologically, to be certain about something, when everything is so uncertain in the world." (24 : 37).

## GROUP NO. 22

### 22-1 (92) INTELLIGENCE

Here is an extremely important key word from the teachings of J. Krishnamurti. By intelligence, we mean the capacity to understand, to store, to remember and to act in an appropriate manner under various situations in life. But this is not the meaning which Krishnamurti ascribes to the word 'intelligence'. He uses the word to mean the freedom to see directly, without the past, without the known. The other words he uses for such direct perception are total attention, understanding, wisdom, seeing, listening, observation without the observer, and so on. Here are some of his important statements:

"Intelligence is the quality of mind that is very sensitive, very alert, very aware. ...It is capable of thinking very clearly, objectively. ...You cannot think clearly if you are prejudiced, if you have opinions. ...Intelligence implies that you see the beauty of the earth, the beauty of the trees, the beauty of the skies, the lovely sunset, the stars, the beauty of subtlety." (9 : 20).

"Intelligence comes into being when you understand the total process of the mind. ...It arises when there is no fear—which means really there is a sense of love." (24 : 224-225).

"What most people call intelligence is merely deftness in some technical activity or cunning in business or political chicanery." (25 : 203).

"Seeing is intelligencc. The only thing you can do is to see. You cannot cultivate intelligence in order to see. Seeing is not the cultivation of intelligence. ...To see means to understand the nature of thought, memory, conflict, ideas; to see all this as a total process is to understand. This is intelligence." (25 : 287).

"Intelligence is not knowledge. If you could read all the books in the world it would not give you intelligence." (29 : 19).

### 22-2 (104) LOVE

There were a few words which Krishnamurti used a very large number of times in his discourses, and he used them in his own peculiar, special style. 'Love' was such a word. To give another example, we may mention the word 'death'. It is very important to understand the meaning of such words which the sage used. We speak of love between mother and child, between husband and wife, between friends or members of an organisation. We speak of a person loving one's nation, language, religion, book, or saint. Krishnamurti does not use the word 'love' in this sense. Let us see from his statements how he has used this key word.

"Freedom and love go together. ...To love is not to ask anything in return, not even to feel that you are giving something—and it is only such love that can know freedom." (24 : 117).

"Through negation of what is not love, love is." (5 : 9).

"That is the extraordinary thing about love: it is the only quality that brings a total comprehension of the whole of existence." (29 : 63).

"In negating what is not love, there is love. You understand, Sirs? You have to negate everything which is not love. Which is: no ambition, no competition, no aggression, no violence either in speech or in act or in thought. ...If you can observe your life, you will find out for yourself what love is." (13 : 11).

"Love can come into being only when there is total self-abandonment. And it is only love that can bring about order, a new culture, a new way of life." (20 : 87).

## 22-3 (124) ORDER

Order and disorder are two extremities of a continuum, like health and disease, peace and uneasiness, gain and loss. One makes for pleasure, harmony, goodwill, the other for pain, obstruction, tension. Krishnamurti has very clearly pointed out an important fact here, namely, that order comes into being negatively, not in a positive manner, by pursuing it positively. Order is established by understanding disorder clearly and completely, which puts an end to disorder. It is most important to understand this fact first. We have already discussed it earlier in **Mahāvākya** No. 6 in Chapter 2, on negation. Here are a few statements of the sage describing order:

"Order is safety, order is harmony, but the very search for order ends in disorder. ...In enlightenment there is order. ...It is when the brain cells reject tribalism, formulas, that in the very rejection is intelligence, which is order." (19 : 141-142).

"I have to think of others. I have to be polite, considerate, be concerned about other people. Out of that consideration, out of that thoughtfulness, out of that watchfulness, both outward and inward, comes order and with that order there comes freedom." (9 : 25).

"In understanding disorder—how each human being creates disorder—in the understanding of that there is a discipline which brings about order." (20 : 64).

## 22-4 (177) UNDERSTANDING

'Understanding' is one of those key words of J. Krishnamurti which stand in need of being explained, because the sage has used it very differently from what it has come to be associated with in the minds of the common people. We associate it with knowledge, memory, retention, recall, and being able to perform properly and appropriately, while Krishnamurti always associated it with attention, seeing, freedom, and self-knowledge. He has explained 'understanding' as given below:

"Knowing is always related to the past and therefore it binds you to the past. Unlike knowing, understanding is not a conclusion, not accumulation. ...Understanding is attention. ...When you attend completely, you understand." (25 : 265).

"Understanding can never be made into a habit, a matter of routine; it demands constant watchfulness, alertness. To understand there must be pliability, sensitivity, a warmth that has nothing to do with sentimentality." (26 : 124).

"Understanding is not an intellectual process. Acquiring knowledge about yourself and learning about yourself are two different things. ...Learning about yourself is not like learning a language or a technology, or a science. ...Then you obviously have to accumulate and remember. ...But in the psychological field learning about yourself is always in the present and knowledge is always in the past. ...Learning is a constant movement without the past. ...Learning implies a great sensitivity." (21 : 22-23).

## 22-5 (184) WISDOM

Wisdom is a key word having almost the same meaning as understanding. The sage has described it as follows:

"There is freedom only in seeing the truth of **what is**, and wisdom is the perception of that truth." (26 : 225).

"To understand oneself is the beginning of wisdom. Wisdom does not lie in books, nor in experience, nor in following another, nor in repeating a lot of platitudes. Wisdom comes to a mind that is understanding itself, understanding how thought is born." (20 : 79).

# GROUP NO. 23

## 23-1 (17) BRAIN

The brain is much larger in proportion to the body weight in man as compared to other living beings. This comparatively large brain size has made it possible to have various capacities of the body and mind, such as classifying sensations, storing their traces, reviving them in the presence of appropriate stimulus, abstract thinking, consciousness of one's own existence, and having emotions, passions and resolutions. All these psychological happenings go on in the billions of cells of the brain and their interconnections called micro-circuits and synapses. They involve different forms of electro-chemical reactions. These reactions go on constantly, and the brain is never totally, wholly silent. Krishnamurti has spoken about the wholly silent state of the brain. The fact of that state of stillness or deep silence may be looked upon as the crux of the whole teaching of the sage. It is only in that state that there is the possibility of coming into being of what he calls understanding, wisdom, self-knowledge, meditation, innocence, sensitivity, simplicity, austerity, benediction, and so on. This is the most remarkable, basic, fundamental and significant revolutionary aspect of his observation, his finding, his outlook, or if we may say so, his philosophy of human life and human mind. Here is how he has described it:

"The real question is whether the brain, the whole of it, can be still, quiet, and respond effectively only when it has to.

...We say it can and this is the understanding of what meditation is." (25 : 280).

"The total brain... must be quiet, speechless, but yet alert and still. There must be no shadow of conflict and imitation. Then there is the astonishing movement called creation." (10 : 48).

"The brain is restless, an astonishingly sensitive instrument. It's always reviving impressions, interpreting them, storing them away. It is never still, waking or sleeping. ...The brain and its activities are a fragment of the totality of life. ...Thought can never understand or formulate the whole of life. Only when the brain and its thoughts are completely still... then only is there the awareness of the whole. ...When time and its measure cease then only is there the whole, the unknowable." (10 : 139-140).

## 23-2 (18) BRAIN CELLS

The sage has said the following about brain cells:

"The question is not how to bring about mutation but to inquire into the structure of the brain cells. ...When there is no movement there is tremendous focus of energy. So mutation is the understanding of movement and the ending of movement in the brain cells themselves." (19 : 39-40).

"The brain cells are the repository of memory. The reaction of memory is thought. Thought can be independent of memory. It is like throwing a stone, which is independent of the hand which throws it." (19 : 163).

"While the brain cells continue to operate they can only operate in the field of knowledge. That is the only thing the brain can do, to function in the field of experience, of knowledge, in the field of time—which is the past." (14 : 96).

## 23-3 (29) CONSCIOUSNESS

The four words, mind, brain, brain cells and consciousness, can be used interchangeably. Krishnamurti has of course used them in that manner. In Sanskrit consciousness is called '**chetanā**' or '**chaitanya**'. A separate, permanent spiritual entity called '**chetana**' is said to be responsible for consciousness in living beings. It is the soul, which leaves the body at death and together with the **chitta**, which is the mind, it enters a new body and there is the birth of a new living being. Krishnamurti does not contribute to this idea of a soul as the entity carrying consciousness from birth to birth. His statements are given below:

"When you become aware of your conditioning you will understand the whole of your consciousness. Consciousness is the total field in which thought functions and relationships exist. All motives, intentions, desires, pleasures, fears, inspirations, hopes, longings, sorrows, joys are in that field." (21 : 29).

"That is our problem, to see the whole of consciousness, not a particular fragment as the conscious or the unconscious. To see the whole of it is one of the most difficult things to do, but to see a fragment is fairly easy." (6 : 22).

"The content of my consciousness is my unhappiness, my misery, my struggles, my sorrows, the images which I have collected through life, my gods, the frustrations, the pleasures, the fears, the agonies, the hatreds—that is my consciousness." (14 : 47).

"Our consciousness is not actually yours or mine; it is the consciousness of man, evolved, grown, accumulated through many, many centuries. In that consciousness is the faith, the gods, all the rituals, man has invented. It is really an activity of thought; it is thought that has made the content—behaviour, action, culture, aspiration. The whole activity of man is the activity of thought." (11 : 32).

## 23-4 (30) CONTENT OF CONSCIOUSNESS

**See under 23-3 (29) CONSCIOUSNESS.**

## 23-5 (59) EXPERIENCE

Experience, experiencing and experiencer are three words used often by the sage in his talks, which we must understand very clearly. Experience is the result of a sensation, which is recognised as 'such and such' by naming and comparing with the past. It is stored in the brain and can be revived by memory. The word 'experiencing' is a key word used by the sage in his own peculiar way. Its meaning is very different from that of 'experience'. It means direct perception, without memory, without naming, without comparison with the past. There is no experiencer taking any part in experiencing. This is a very important fact brought out by Krishnamurti, which must never be lost sight of. The experiencer means the 'me', the self, the ego, the thinker, which is a fictitious entity arising due to the use of language, words as symbols. The sage has stressed the difference between 'experience' and 'experiencing' in the statements given below:

"In seeking experience lies the way to illusion. Not to seek any form of experience is very difficult; most of our lives are so mechanical, so shallow, that we want deeper experiences, because we are bored with the superficiality of life. We want or rather crave for something that will have a meaning, a fullness, depth, beauty, loveliness, and so the mind is seeking." (6 : 124).

"According to my memories I react to whatever I see, to whatever I feel. In this process of reacting to what I see, what I feel, what I know, what I believe, experience is taking place, is it not? Reaction, response to something seen, is experience." (24 : 52).

"Experience is not the means to experiencing, which is a state without experience. Experience must cease for experiencing to be. ...In the state of experiencing there is neither the experiencer nor the experienced." (26 : 32).

## 23-6 (97) KNOWLEDGE

**See under Mahāvākya No. 4, Chapter 2.**

## 23-7 (98) KNOWN

**See under Mahāvākya No. 4, Chapter 2.**

## 23-8 (108) MEMORY

The capacity to store experiences in the brain cells and revive them when needed is a necessity in human life for dealing successfully and adequately with various situations. In human beings two factors have contributed to this capacity, called memory. They are: the comparatively large brain size, and the use of words as symbols. But this capacity has no use, no place, in direct perception, understanding, or wisdom. This is made clear by Krishnamurti in the following statements:

"Memory is always in the past, and the memory is given life in the present by a challenge. Memory has no life in itself. It comes to life in the present when confronted by a challenge. All memory, whether dormant or active, is conditioned." (24 : 32).

"Of course memory has a place at a certain level. In everyday life we could not function at all without it. In its own field it must be efficient, but there is a state of mind where it has very little place. A mind which is not crippled by memory has real freedom." (21 : 36).

"Experience is memory, and without word, symbol, image, there is no memory. ...Experiencing is direct. Then relationship is direct, and not through memory. It is this direct relationship that brings understanding." (26 : 109).

## 23-9 (109) MIND

**See under 27-2 (78) HUMAN MIND.**

## 23-10 (129) PAST

**See under Mahāvākya No. 4, Chapter 2.**

## 23-11 (168) THOUGHT

The capacity to think about various things in their absence, i.e., abstract thinking, is a special capacity of human beings which has helped them to be the most developed and powerful (psychologically) among all living beings. But thought received a severe beating at the hands of J. Krishnamurti, because he observed that it comes in the way of direct perception and thereby hampers the state of understanding and wisdom. This fact is the very backbone of the world view of the sage. It is an extremely significant finding. Here are some of his statements explaining this subtle and remarkable finding.

"Thought invests in belief, to protect itself against fear which it has brought into being. And the way of thought is not the freedom of attention which sees truth. ...The negation of thought is attention as the negation of thought is love." (25 : 57).

"Thought in its very nature is divisive. It is thought that seeks pleasure and holds it. It is thought that cultivates desire." (25 : 238).

"Thought tries to sustain pleasure and thereby nourishes fear. ...Thought engenders loneliness but condemns it and so invents ways of escaping from it, through various forms of religious or cultural entertainment, through the everlasting search for deeper and wider dependencies. ...Thought has created a centre as the 'me'—my opinion, my country, my God, my experience, my house, my wife. ...That is the centre from which you act." (6 : 67-68).

"Thought itself, in itself, is of the past, and therefore it is not free, it is always old. ...Thought organises our life, based on the past. ...It projects what should be tomorrow, and so there is conflict." (14 : 68).

## 23-12 (172) TRADITION

**See under Mahāvākya No. 4, Chapter 2.**

## GROUP NO. 24

## 24-1 (112) MUTATION

## 24-2 (139) REGENERATION

## 24-3 (143) REVOLUTION

## 24-4 (174) TRANSFORMATION

**See all the above categories under Mahāvākya No. 1, Chapter 2.**

## GROUP NO. 25

## 25-1 (53) ENDING OF SORROW

Every one of us desires freedom from sorrow and a state which is ever untouched by sorrow. We like to believe strongly in the existence of such a state and we like to also believe that in the past there have been human beings (called the **jivanmuktas**) who had attained such a state 'untouched by sorrow' in their life.

Krishnamurti's treatment of sorrow is different from such a belief. He has stressed the need to perceive it, to look at or see it, directly, without any escape or running away, without a desire to change it, justify it or condemn it. With such direct understanding alone can sorrow end, and with the ending of sorrow there is also the ending of thought, the 'me', and of time. Here are the original statements of the sage:

"In ending sorrow, time must come to an end. Sorrow cannot end by thought. When time stops, thought as the way of sorrow ceases. It is thought and time that divide and separate." (25 : 105).

"Knowing oneself is the ending of sorrow. ...To end sorrow is to see the fact and not invent its opposite, for the opposites contain each other." (25 : 247).

"The ending of sorrow is the ending of time." (10 : 113).

"Only in observing without the observer, who is the past, does one see the nature of time and the ending of time." (11 : 41).

"When you understand the structure of your daily living—with its competition, greed, ambition, and the search for power—then you will see not only the absurdities of theories, saviours and gurus, but you may find the ending to sorrow, an ending to the whole structure which thought has put together." (25 : 13).

## 25-2 (54) ENDING OF THOUGHT

**See under 25-1 (53) ENDING OF SORROW.**

## 25-3 (55) ENDING OF TIME

**See under 25-1 (53) ENDING OF SORROW.**

## GROUP NO. 26

### 26-1 (56) ENERGY

Seeing, looking, direct perception, understanding, knowing oneself, wisdom are states which, as Krishnamurti has pointed out a number of times, require tremendous energy. He has brought out the importance of silence or stillness of the mind for focusing of energy, and stopping the waste of energy caused by conflict. Here is what he has actually said:

"One needs abundant energy to find truth, and this energy is dissipated through the conflict which results from suppression, conformity, compulsion. But yielding to desire also breeds self-contradiction, which again dissipates energy." (28 : 294).

"Total energy does not come about through abstinence, through the vows of chastity and poverty, for all determination and action of will is waste of energy because thought is involved in it, and thought is wasted energy; perception never is." (25 : 117).

"If you are prepared to let go, then what takes place? Which means you let go the talent, the fulfilment, the perpetuation of the 'me'. Now when does this mutation in the brain cells through energy take place? You see, where energy is being dissipated through talent and through other channels, energy is not completely held. When this energy has no movement at all, then I think something happens, then it must explode. I think then the quality of the brain cells itself changes. ...When there is no movement inwardly or outwardly, when there is no demand for experience, no awakening, no seeking, no movement of any kind, then energy is at its height. Which means one must negate all movement. When that takes place, energy is completely quiet, which is silence." (19 : 38).

### 26-2 (127) PASSION

This is a word which Krishnamurti has used for 'total energy', which brings enlightenment or understanding. He has described passion as follows:

"We have no passion. We have lust, we have pleasure. The root meaning of the word 'passion' is sorrow. ...When we remain with sorrow totally... then you will find, out of that sorrow comes passion. That passion has the quality of love, and love has no sorrow." (14 : 81).

"When the mind is sensitive, there is no centre, there is no 'me' in it... it is intensely passionate and it is such a mind that sees what is beautiful. ...Suffering is a partial activity of energy. It is a fragmentary energy. ...When there is no activity of the fragment, there is complete focusing of all energy. ...If there is a harmonious whole, that energy is passion. The 'me' as the past is completely dissolved and therefore such a mind is full of energy and passion, and therefore that is beauty." (19 : 151).

"You can't find any truth without passion. ...I don't know what significance you give to it, the feeling of complete passion, with a fury behind it, with total energy, that passion in which there is no hidden want." (14 : 198).

## GROUP NO. 27

### 27-1 (77) HUMAN LIFE

All of us go through our life as human beings, but very few of us may be aware of the vast variety of aspects human life has got. Our interest, our awareness, and our inquiry is limited, superficial, and rather half-hearted. Krishnamurti was an observer **par excellence** of the world around us in general and of human life in particular. He has described his keen and passionate observations in a superbly vivid manner in his writings. Some of them are reproduced below:

"What does life mean? Is not life an extraordinary thing? The birds, the flowers, the flourishing trees, the heavens, the stars, the rivers, and the fish therein—all this is life. Life is the poor, and the rich, life is the constant battle between groups, races, and nations, life is meditation, life is what we call religion, and it is also the subtle, hidden things of the mind—the envies, the ambitions, the passions, the fears, fulfilments and anxieties. All this and much more is life. We generally prepare ourselves to understand only one small corner of it." (24 : 93).

"Life is everything—study, play, sex, work, quarrels, envy, ambition, love, beauty, truth. But most of us have not the patience, earnestly and consistently to pursue this inquiry." (24 : 225).

## 27-2 (78) HUMAN MIND

We live in a world in which experts and specialists have a great importance and an extremely useful role to play. If we would describe Krishnamurti as an expert or specialist, then what shall we say about his field of expertise and specialty? Obviously he was a great epoch-making specialist of 'the ways of the human mind'. There is no doubt about that. The working of the human mind was, indeed, his field of specialty. That would be very clear from his following statements:

"Can the mind cease to be? That is the problem. Mind, as we know it, has belief behind it, has desire, the urge to be secure, knowledge, and accumulation of strength. ...In the mind is the very essence which creates contradiction, which isolates and separates." (24 : 41).

"The human mind wants permanency in everything—in relationship, in property, in virtue. It wants something which cannot be destroyed. That is why we say God is permanent or truth is absolute." (24 : 192).

"We carry on like machines with our tiresome daily routine. How eagerly the mind accepts a pattern of existence, and how tenaciously it clings to it! As by a driven nail, the mind is held together by an idea, and around the idea it lives and has its being. The mind is never free, pliable, for it is always anchored; it moves within the radius, narrow or wide, of its own centre. From its centre it dare not wander; and when it does, it is lost in fear." (27 : 96-97).

"A mind that is the result of time, a mind that has read, studied, that has meditated upon what it has been taught, and is in itself continuance of the past—how can such a mind experience reality, the timeless, the ever new? How can it ever fathom the unknown? Surely, to know, to be certain, is the way of vanity, arrogance." (29 : 100).

"To observe the mind—this mind that chatters, that projects ideas, that lives in contradiction, in constant conflict and compulsion—I must obviously be very quiet... I must give attention, I cannot be chattering. ...The mind must be attentive, must be silent, quiet." (6 : 91).

## 27-3 (80) HOW

One very significant difference between J. Krishnamurti and the other sages was that he never advocated any method for enlightenment, understanding, freedom, wisdom, or self-knowledge, whereas many others who were his contemporaries had their own special method for attaining the ultimate spiritual goal. They were all taken to be experts, masters, of 'how to reach there'. Krishnamurti always shunned the 'how'. He urged that there was no method, no way, no path, to truth or reality. The 'how' was a projection of the conditioned mind. This is a very subtle, rather difficult-to-grasp point which must be understood very clearly in its proper perspective. In science and technology, in learning any art or skill, the 'how to do it' has an important place which cannot be ignored or avoided. But the state of freedom, understanding, self-knowing can never be the outcome or result of a method, an effort, or a discipline, strife. Here are Krishnamurti's own words explaining this important point:

"Our education is in formulas and conclusions. The 'how' is the demand for a formula, but formulas cannot resolve the problem. Please understand the truth of this. It is only when we do not seek inward security that we can live outwardly secure." (27 : 112).

"The 'how' implies gradual freedom, but confusion cannot be cleared bit by bit. ...The 'how' implies a gradual achievement of freedom, which is only the action of confusion." (28 : 50-51).

"That is one of the most destructive questions: 'tell me how'. Man has always been saying throughout the world, 'tell me how'. If you see a snake, a poisonous cobra, you do not say, 'Please tell me how to run away from it'. You run away from it." (9 : 17).

## 27-4 (93) INTENTION TO FIND OUT

One very sad fact about J. Krishnamurti's endeavour throughout his life—"to set man absolutely, unconditionally free"—was that it was made wholly inconsequential by all of us, because our intention to find out, to understand, has always been very meagre. So all his talks and discourses fell on deaf ears; his words could never penetrate our barren, dry, unenergetic hearts, and there was never any inner change in any one of us. Obviously, the sage knew this fact very clearly. This is seen from what he said in the statements reproduced below:

"To discover there must be the intention, the search, the inquiry. So long as that intention to find out, to inquire deeply, is weak or does not exist, mere assertion or a casual wish to find out about oneself is of very little significance." (24 : 23).

"If you will experiment with what I have been saying, you will find that there is immediate regeneration, a newness, a quality of freshness; because the mind is always still when it is interested, when it desires or has the intention to understand. The difficulty with most of us is that we have not the intention to understand." (24 : 89).

"In order to observe the movement of your own mind and heart, of your whole being, you must have a free mind, not a mind that agrees and disagrees, taking sides in an argument, disputing over mere words, but rather following with an intention to understand—a very difficult thing to do because most of us don't know how to look at, or listen to, our own being any more than we know how to look at the beauty of a river or listen to the breeze among the trees." (21 : 23-24).

## 27-5 (94) INTENTION TO UNDERSTAND

**See under 27-4 (93) INTENTION TO FIND OUT.**

## 27-6 (140) RELATIONSHIP

Relationship with people, things, events, and ideas—this is our life according to Krishnamurti. He looks upon relationship as a mirror in which we can see ourselves as we are, as we actually live our life. Such observation yields self-knowledge, which is the beginning of wisdom. This point has been stressed repeatedly by the sage. Here are his actual words:

"To **be** is to be related, and there is no such thing as living in isolation. ...The world is our relationship, however narrow; and if we can bring a transformation there, not a superficial but a radical transformation, then we shall begin actively to transform the world." (24 : 22).

"To understand myself, I must understand relationship. Relationship is a mirror in which I can see myself. That mirror can either be distorted or it can be 'as is', reflecting 'that which is'...We do not see **what is**. We would rather idealise, escape, we would rather live in the future than understand that relationship in the immediate present." (24 : 77).

"If you can look into the mirror of relationship exactly as you look into the ordinary mirror, then there is no end to self-knowledge. It is like entering a fathomless ocean which has no shore. ...If you can just observe what you are, and move with it, then you will find that it is possible to go infinitely far. Then there is no end to the journey, and that is the mystery, the beauty of it." (29 : 43).

## 27-7 (149) SECOND HAND

A second-hand thing is that which is already used by another person. Second-hand knowledge means ideas and information borrowed from others without experience. Most of our knowledge in life is learned from others. But all of that is not second-hand knowledge. That part of it which we can handle, deal with, put to use on our own can be called first-hand knowledge. For example, techniques, arts, and skills. We can teach them to others and we can be said to have originality in them. But those beliefs which we have accepted in the religious and spiritual fields, of which we do not have any experience, yet we hold them, and very firmly—such beliefs are second-hand ideas. Krishnamurti calls him a second-hand person who entertained beliefs on the authority of scriptures, gurus, tradition, without having any insight or first-hand experience. Most of us are like that in certain fields. That is one great contributing factor to so much conflict and misery in human life. This is explained by the sage in the following statements:

"All our knowledge is second hand, our traditions are second hand; there may perhaps be a few activities that are totally our own and not of another. So, are we aware that it is our direct perception and not second-hand knowledge learnt from another?" (14 : 312).

"For centuries we have been spoon-fed by our teachers, by our authorities, by our books, our saints. ...We live on words and our life is shallow and empty. We are second-hand people. ...We are the result of all kinds of influences and there is nothing new in us, nothing that we have discovered for ourselves, nothing original, pristine, clear." (21 : 10).

"If you learn from yourself about yourself then you will not be a second-hand human being." (9 : 14).

## 27-8 (157) SELF-PITY

In the face of a calamity the suffering mind puts the blame on bad luck, on being unfortunate, being troubled by others for nothing. This is self-pity. It is a sort of complaining attitude, holding 'fate' responsible for misery and sorrow. Krishnamurti has pointed out that lack of self-knowledge gives rise to self-pity. Here are his own words:

"Meditation is never prayer. Prayer, supplication is born of self-pity. You pray when you are in difficulty, when there is sorrow. ...This self-pity so deeply embedded in man is the root of separation. ...Out of this confusion one cries to heaven ...or to some deity of the mind." (25 : 106).

"Self-pity is one of the elements of sorrow. ...The trouble is the utter lack of knowing oneself. Knowing oneself is the ending of sorrow." (25 : 247).

## 27-9 (162) SORROW

Human life is beset with joy and sorrow. Both are reactions of the human mind to happenings in life. It is a natural, ingrained tendency of the human mind to crave the former and to run away, try to escape from the latter. The avoidance of sorrow, pain, misery, has been a primary concern of philosophy, religion, and practically every human endeavour. Krishnamurti has discussed ending of sorrow through perceiving it directly, facing it without an escape, through knowing oneself with total attention. His statements are reproduced below:

"Sorrow has to be understood and not ignored. ...To understand suffering, there must be no positive action of the mind to justify or to overcome it, the mind must be entirely passive, silently watchful so that it can follow without hesitation the unfolding of sorrow. ...There must be suffering as long as there is no understanding of the ways of the self; and the ways of the self are to be discovered only in the action of relationship." (26 : 236-237).

"How can the mind resolve the factor of sorrow? Not through **ātman**. That is too childish. It can only resolve it, not through knowledge, but by looking at it without knowledge." (19 : 186).

## 27-10 (169) TIME

Like sorrow, truth, reality, time has been a subject in which philosophers have always taken a very keen interest. They have spoken about a timeless state like the **ātman**, **brahman**, and God, and have tirelessly and passionately discussed how one can achieve it, realise it, or reach it in life. Krishnamurti has pointed out two kinds of time, the chronological, and the psychological. The former is a necessity; the latter, he has said, is an illusion. Why does he call it an illusion? It is because freedom, self-knowledge, wisdom, understanding, cannot be realised, attained, step by step, i.e., by making progress with the passage of time. Enlightenment takes place instantaneously, all of a sudden, through passive awareness, direct perception, looking, seeing. This fact is pointed out by the sage thus:

"There are two kinds of time, the chronological and the psychological. There is time as yesterday by the watch and as yesterday by memory. You cannot reject chronological time; it would be absurd—you would miss your train. ...Psychological time is a product of the mind." (24 : 86).

"Time is necessary in the realm of achieving, gaining, becoming proficient in some profession, in a career that demands training. There, time seems not only necessary but must exist. And in the world of the psyche this same movement, this becoming, is extended. ...The religious, the evolutionary books, have informed us that we need time to change from '**what is**' to 'what should be'. The distance covered is time. ...Perhaps that is one of the miseries of man—in the hope of fulfilment, and the pain that fulfilment, that hope, is not achieved, is not come by easily." (11 : 51).

## 27-11 (179) VIOLENCE

**See under Mahāvākya No. 1, Chapter 2.**

## 27-12 (187) YOU ARE THE WORLD

Krishnamurti has spoken about a kind of unity, oneness, between the individual and society, the world around. He said that all of us have a brain which has evolved over millions of years. Beliefs and emotions are seen to be shared by all. So individuals are not separate, but there is sharing of qualities among all of them. But we have the habit of looking at ourselves as separate, unique, different, from the world, having a separate existence. This is, actually, the feeling of 'me', the self, the thinker, the individual. This feeling, as Krishnamurti looks at it, is an illusion, a projection of the mind. This point is stressed in the following statements:

"You, Sir, are the rest of humanity, psychologically, deeply. Your reactions are shared by all humanity. Your brain is not yours, it has evolved through centuries of time. ...We are questioning deeply whether there is an individual at all. We are the whole of humanity; we are the rest of mankind. This is not a romantic, fantastic statement, and it is important, necessary." (11 : 30).

"I think one has to understand, not as a theory, not as a speculative, entertaining concept, but rather as an actual fact—that we are the world and the world is us. The world is each one of us; to feel that, to be really committed to it and to nothing else, brings about a feeling of great responsibility and an action that must not be fragmentary, but whole." (14 : 75).

# BIBLIOGRAPHY

1. A Wholly Different Way of Living. J. Krishnamurti in dialogue with Professor Allen W. Anderson. Chennai: 2000, K.F.I.

2. Cadogan, Mary et al. (Ed.), Total Freedom—The Essential Krishnamurti, New York: 1996, HarperCollins Publ. Inc.

3. Jaykar, Pupul, J. Krishnamurti—a Biography. Harmondsworth: 1986, Penguin Books.

4. Joshi, Kalidas, Understanding J. Krishnamurti, New Delhi: 2002, Rupa and Co.

5. Krishnamurti, J., A Dialogue With Oneself, Madras: 1995, K.F.I.

6. Krishnamurti, J., Beyond Violence, Bombay: 1973, B.I. Publ.

7. Krishnamurti, J., Conversations, New Delhi: 1975, Orient Longman Ltd.

8. Krishnamurti, J., Freedom, Responsibility and Discipline, Madras: 1995, K.F.I.

9. Krishnamurti, J., Krishnamurti on Education, New Delhi: 1974, Orient Longman Ltd.

10. Krishnamurti, J., Krishnamurti's Notebook, London: 1977, Victor Gollancz Ltd.

11. Krishnamurti, J., Krishnamurti to Himself (His Last Journal) London: 1987, Victor Gollancz Ltd.

12. Krishnamurti, J., Life Ahead, London: 1964, Victor Gollancz.

13. Krishnamurti, J., Mind in Meditation, Madras: 1995, K.F.I.

14. Krishnamurti, J., The Awakening of Intelligence, London: 1973, Victor Gollancz Ltd.

**15.** Krishnamurti, J., The Book of Life, Madras: 1975, K.F.I.

**16.** Krishnamurti, J., The First and Last Freedom, Chennai: 2001, K.F.I.

**17.** Krishnamurti, J., The Wholeness of Life, London: 1978, Victor Gollancz Ltd.

**18.** Krishnamurti, J., Time and the Timeless, Madras: 1977, K.F.I.

**19.** Krishnamurti, J., Tradition and Revolution, Pune: 1974, Sangam Press.

**20.** Krishnamurti, K (compiler), Krishnamurti for Beginners, Madras: 1995, K.F.I.

**21.** Lutyens, Mary (Ed.), Freedom from the Known (by J. Krishnamurti), New Delhi: 1987, K.F.I.

**22.** Lutyens, Mary, Krishnamurti—His Life and Death, New York: 1991, Avon Books.

**23.** Lutyens, Mary, Krishnamurti—The Years of Awakening, London: 1975, John Murray.

**24.** Lutyens, Mary, (Ed.), The Penguin Krishnamurti Reader, Harmondsworth: 1974, Penguin Books.

**25.** Lutyens, Mary, (Ed.), The Second Penguin Krishnamurti Reader, Harmondsworth: 1974, Penguin Books.

**26.** Rajgopal, D., (Ed.), Commentaries on Living (From the notebook of J. Krishnamurti), New Delhi: 1974, B.I. Publ.

**27.** Rajgopal, D., (Ed.), Commentaries on Living (From the notebook of J. Krishnamurti), II series, New Delhi: 1974, B.I. Publ.

**28.** Rajgopal, D., (Ed.), Commentaries on Living (From the notebook of J. Krishnamurti), III series, New Delhi: 1974, B.I. Publ.

**29.** Rajgopal, D. (Ed.), This Matter of Culture (By J. Krishnamurti), London: 1964, Victor Gollancz Ltd.

**30.** Sloss, Radha Rajgopal, Lives in the Shadow With J. Krishnamurti, London: 1991, Bloomsbury Publ. Ltd.

# INDEX

## E



## F



## G



## H



## I



## J

## Q



## R



## S



## T

# Pearls of Spiritual Wisdom

*—Dr Aparna Chattopadhyay*

In your quiet moments of introspection are you often nagged by the feeling that your life seems to be an endless struggle for happiness, much like chasing a mirage? Do you wish to be calm, cool and collected, with an inner peace at all times? Do you wish to transform your life into a blissful success story?

Then read this practical guide to everyday spirituality and empower yourself by contemplating and comprehending the basic truths of life, such as:

- ❖ Who are you?
- ❖ Why are you here?
- ❖ Why has human life been given to you?
- ❖ What is the true art of living?
- ❖ How do you unleash your latent spiritual qualities?
- ❖ How do you experience causeless love and ceaseless joy?
- ❖ How do you live powerfully and spiritually?

...And many more intriguing questions. Living in spirituality has therapeutic value, as the latest medical research reveals. When sound in spirituality, you become less prone to emotional and physical disorders, since your inner system is fortified and better attuned to withstand the tensions of present-day living. Make spiritual ideals a practical part of daily living for success, happiness and bliss to be your handmaidens forever.

---

***Demy Size • Pages: 158***
***Price: Rs. 80/- • Postage: Rs. 15/-***

---

# Know the Vedas At a Glance

—*Dr. Raj Kumar,* PhD

***A clear and concise account on select aspects of the Vedas to gain true knowledge, solve problems of every kind and ensure peace, prosperity and happiness.***

The scriptures and classics of a nation are its true heritage, laying a firm foundation for its people to follow. The Vedas are India's and the world's oldest scripture, believed to have been directly revealed by God.

Know the Vedas at a Glance gives a clear and concise account on select aspects of the Vedas, which help dispel ignorance, superstition and false beliefs. The Vedas are replete with guidelines to solve varied problems – social, economic, political, scientific, mental or any other. The message of the Vedas holds relevance for the layman as well as scientists, politicians, educationists, parents and people of every hue. Understanding and following the essence of the Vedas ensures a happy, healthy, peaceful and prosperous life.

***Demy Size • Pages: 136***
***Price: Rs. 80/- • Postage: Rs. 15/-***

# Freedom from Thought

*—Ashok Gollerkeri*

***Don't let your Negative thoughts rule you***

The book contains 50 spiritual essays which focus on joys and sorrows, triumphs and tragedies, spontaneity and complexities of human life. It also focuses on the universal nature of the challenges of human life, transcending all man-made barriers. Ashok examines the eternal thirst for lasting peace and joy, and the nature of the journey for self-discovery. A single reading of the book will transform your life. You will start realising how fortunate you are to have the gift of life and possess all that you do, rather than hanker for what you don't have!

---

***Demy size • Pages: 168***
***Price: Rs. 96/- • Postage: Rs. 15/-***

---

# Dehypnotic Meditation

*—Yogiraj Nanak*

***The Door to a Voyage into the Infinite***

Dehypnotic Meditation – The Door to a Voyage into the Infinite is a refreshing and definitive guide to this most popular subject. It leads the reader gently but firmly through the different stages of meditation up to the ultimate experience. It is authored by Swami Yogiraj, the 14th spiritual descendent to the seat of the 16th century saint-poet, Baba Maluk Das of Kada, Allahabad, India.

The book explains the working of the mind and how to go beyond it and discover the source of joy and wisdom within. The book covers all aspects of meditation – psychological, philosophical and spiritual – and provides practical guidance to beginners and experts alike. Answers are provided on how to: command the subconscious mind; keep away negative thoughts; develop the aura; perform self-healing; break old habits and enter into Divine Romance.

---

***Demy Size • Pages: 136***
***Price: Rs. 96/- • Postage: Rs. 15/-***

---

# The Yoga of GITA

*—Dr Ram Shanker Tiwari*

***Scriptural guidelines to success, serenity, harmony & happiness***

The Bhagavad Gita is replete with universal wisdom and the techniques to attain this. The Yoga of Gita contains the essence of this wisdom, the philosophy of creation and the Ultimate Reality, as revealed by Sri Krishna to Arjuna. The book outlines the various paths for realisation. For the layman, the emphasis is on the Yoga of Action – acting without worrying about the rewards for our actions.

The book is a rendition of the 18 chapters, retold in simple language, with a brief account on Yoga and Meditation, which will ensure success, serenity, harmony and happiness for readers who follow these principles, finally leading to Salvation.

***Demy Size • Pages: 156***
***Price: Rs. 80/- • Postage: Rs. 15/-***

# How to Integrate the SELF

*—Nitin Orayan*

***Harmonise your Body, Mind & Soul***

The way you live, the work you do, and minor and major matters in your life can either make you an integrated person – fulfilled, content and complete – or do just the opposite, leaving you dissatisfied, disenchanted and frustrated. Experiencing 'completeness' or 'wholeness' of being has much to do with living in the present moment that you are experiencing NOW – a moment that will soon pass, never to return.

How to Integrate the Self teaches the reader ways to fully utilise and enjoy every moment of life by revealing the true meaning of existence. The book guides the reader on how to flow with one's life and let all of life's little changes happen as one coasts along, thereby discovering the true joy of living and the pure lightness of being.

***Demy size • Pages: 112***
***Price: Rs. 80/- • Postage: Rs. 15/-***